Free Association

Free Association

Method and Process

ANTON O. KRIS

NEW HAVEN AND LONDON
YALE UNIVERSITY PRESS

Published with assistance from the Mary Cady Tew Memorial Fund.

The author gratefully acknowledges permission from
The Psychoanalytic Study of the Child to quote from
his article: "Either-Or Dilemmas," first published in
volume 32, 1977; and from Alfred A. Knopf, Inc., for
permission to quote from *The Collected Poems of
Wallace Stevens*, 1954.

Designed by James J. Johnson
and set in Melior Roman.
Printed in the United States of America by
Edwards Brothers Inc., Ann Arbor, Mich.

Library of Congress Cataloging in Publication Data

Kris, Anton O., 1934–
  Free association.

  Bibliography: p.
  Includes index.
    1. Free association (Psychology)   2. Psycho-
analysis. I. Title. [DNLM: 1. Free association.
WM 460.5.F8 K92f]
RC506.K74   616.89'17   81–11562
ISBN O–300–02733–8   AACR2

10   9   8   7   6   5   4   3   2   1

I do not know which to prefer,
The beauty of inflections
Or the beauty of innuendoes,
The blackbird whistling
Or just after.

WALLACE STEVENS
from "Thirteen Ways of Looking at a Blackbird"

Contents

Preface

In this book I try to describe the way I understand psychoanalysis and the way I practice it. I believe that our method and our data are better than our formulations of psychoanalytic technique. The literature of psychoanalysis contains a myriad of nuanced clinical descriptions and an endless array of magnificent expressions of human wisdom. Yet for the individual seeking to develop the capacity to use the psychoanalytic method—whether in psychoanalysis proper or in one of its derivative therapies—the task of organizing the methods, data, and theories of others into a synthesis of his own remains formidable and, at times, forbidding.

Accordingly, I present a way of going about that task, by focusing on free association as method. My aim is to illustrate the initial formulation of the psychoanalytic process and its elements in terms of the method of free association. I hope thereby to facilitate research into the role of theory and formulation in the practice of psychoanalysis and psychotherapy. I make no attempt, however, to illustrate every aspect of technique or of free association.

Among the fields in which the psychoanalytic literature is especially rich, for obvious reasons, are its discussions and illustrations of free association. At one time I had expected to begin this volume with an extensive review. Now, Patrick Mahony (1979) has placed me permanently in his debt by providing such a review, far more scholarly and complete than I would have prepared. He cites and discusses the contributions of many who have enriched our understanding of free association. Nonetheless, I wish to sketch briefly the place of free association in the history of psychoanalytic technique, as it has gradually developed from its beginnings in "chimney sweeping" under hypnosis (Breuer and Freud, 1893–95) over the past hundred years.

Once Freud had abandoned hypnosis, which he regarded as his "most momentous step" (1924, p. 195), he first made use of directed free association, with physical and verbal influences on the doctor's part to set the course. The aim was to recover buried memories and to facilitate abreaction of strangulated affect. Resistance and transference were formulated narrowly, as obstacles to therapeutic remembering. Later, considerations of symbolic representation, of unconscious mental mechanisms, and of psychological development from infancy to adulthood culminated in the synthesis of *The Interpretation of Dreams* (1900), where free association holds a preeminent position as the method of investigation. The use of directed free association in regard to isolated elements of the manifest dream retains something of the character of the earlier approach, but it differs from Freud's earliest psychoanalytic technique in that the directive influence is the patient's own dream. Kinds and qualities of thinking and a systematic psychology of conflict were formulated in *The Interpretation of Dreams* in genetic, dynamic, topographic, and economic terms closely linked to the functions of free association. For several years that model served to foster new research.

Gradually, interest focused on character and character pathology, on its origins in early childhood relationships, and on their reproduction in the transference. New and fruitful theoretical formulations accompanied this shift of interest. These formulations, however, were increasingly distant from free association, although the technique of free association and the fundamental rule that required the patient to report on his mental activity without bias or selection continued to serve as the main vehicle of communication. On the whole, the psychoanalytic treatment process has come to be seen in theoretical terms, in terms of a complex structural theory of the mind and its development (Freud, 1923). Analysis of resistance and transference, now defined in terms of mental structures and their functions, is regarded as the major vehicle of the treatment, while free association serves as the somewhat neglected handmaiden to those theoretical stepsisters.

In this book I illustrate an alternative approach to clinical formulation, which focuses on free association not only as the source of data but as the point of departure for formulation. It follows Freud's emphasis upon "the technique of free association, considered by many people the most important contribution made by psychoanalysis, the methodological key to its results" (1931, p. 403).

The approach I present in no way disputes the value or significance of theory. On the contrary, I find psychoanalytic theory indispensable in my work. What is in question is not the usefulness of theory but how and when it is to be applied to the data in the clinical situation. I suggest that much is to be gained—at least I have found it so—in formulating clinical data from the viewpoint of the method with which they are obtained, the method of free association. That method includes not only the patient's attempts to report what is on his mind but also the analyst's interventions, influenced by his temperament and by his clinical experience and theoretical understanding. Initial formulation of clinical data in terms of the method rather than in terms of a theoretical conception of the mind may help the analyst to study his application of theory and to evaluate the theory he uses as each intervention reflects the influence of conceptual formulation, explicit or implicit.

I have profited from the work of several authors whose explicit aim has been to approach psychoanalytic work from a methodological point of view. I have in mind, especially, Hermann (1934), Rapaport (1944), Klein (1976), and Schafer (1976, 1978). My views share many points in common with each of theirs, as theirs do among themselves.

In the pages that follow I refer to the published literature sparingly. The reader should take for granted that every observation I discuss can be found in earlier published descriptions. Freud said a great deal about free association and the psychoanalytic method. Others, especially Loewenstein (1981), have expanded upon his writings, added to them, and brought them up to date (Greenson, 1967; Gray, 1973; Blum, 1979). There is very little if anything original in the observations I offer.

As to my approach to free association—that is what I bring to market. Here the early influence of operant methods in my psychological training shows through. The way I approach the

free association method, the way I relate observations, theoretical formulations, and psychoanalytic technique differs somewhat from the way I was taught psychoanalysis. Like every
other psychoanalyst, I have had to make my own synthesis. It
remains to be seen how well or how little it may suit others as a
contribution to their own.

Acknowledgments

This book draws heavily upon the work of teachers and colleagues. Their number, beginning with my father, has grown too large for naming. I want therefore to express my appreciation to them collectively before turning to those who have made particular contributions to these pages.

For over five years I have had the opportunity to participate in enormously stimulating group discussions of clinical psychoanalysis with Drs. Gerald Adler, Howard A. Corwin, Ralph P. Engle, Arthur R. Kravitz, Charles E. Magraw, and S. Joseph Nemetz. Many of the ideas that animate this book first surfaced in that tolerant atmosphere. Their many valuable suggestions on the manuscript have been gratefully incorporated.

Drs. Peter B. Neubauer and Albert J. Solnit, with characteristic generosity, read the manuscript as soon as it was in their hands. The book and its author have benefited greatly from the wisdom of their penetrating criticism and judicious recommendations. Helpful comments came also from Drs. Sanford Gifford, Ernest L. Hartmann, Roger L. Shapiro, and Julius Silberger. Continuing a collaboration of several years, Mrs. Lottie M. Newman edited the final draft of the manuscript. I am grateful for her unparalleled experience and judgment.

Both because this book attempts to illustrate the way I personally practice psychoanalysis and because I am grammatically a child of my time, references to "the analyst" are followed by the masculine pronoun. The book and its author, however, owe much to women colleagues. My wife, Dr. Kathryn B. Kris, has helped to shape my ideas over the years. She was the first reader of every line and also the one on whose judgment I relied, finally, for every revision. My sister, Dr. Anna K. Wolff, read the manuscript at several stages, improving it at many crucial points both in content and in form. My mother, Dr. Marianne Kris, who long encouraged me to write about the technique of psychoanalysis and psychotherapy, gave every page the extraordinary benefit of more than fifty years' experience as an analyst. That she was pleased with it remains for me a source of enduring satisfaction, for this is her book.

Free Association

1

Formulation from the Viewpoint of Free Association

Psychoanalysts regularly emphasize the interaction of theory and technique. The way we formulate, the way we make abstractions from observation and the way we relate evidence and inference, reflects and influences what we do in analyzing. Psychoanalytic theories of the mind, which have proven their usefulness in a number of contexts, have left considerable room for improvement as the basis for understanding the conduct and process of psychoanalytic treatment. Many questions remain unanswered in regard to the application of psychoanalytic theories in the clinical context. This book provides one possible answer, by focusing on initial formulations of the analytic process relatively free of theories of the mind. In placing a central emphasis on the method of free association and on observation of free associations, it temporarily bypasses, though it does not obviate, the need for a theory of the mind. Its governing principle is more closely connected with the distinction between experience-near and experience-distant psychoanalytic formulation (Waelder, 1962) than with the distinction between clinical and metapsychological theories.

Characteristically, psychoanalytic theories focus upon the patient's behavior or the patient's mind, from a variety of points of view. The statement of these theories, however, regularly omits consideration of differences among the analysts who are to apply them. While theoretical formulations in general may be employed more explicitly by some analysts, more implicitly by others, it is not hard to demonstrate that psychoanalysts differ in predilection for particular kinds of theoretical formulation. What is figure for one may well be background for another. Therefore, correct application of theory is deter-

1

mined not only by observations of the patient's behavior and state of mind but by the way the analyst uses theoretical formulation to organize his understanding and his interventions. Selection of theoretical perspective is one element in the analyst's participation in the analytic process.

While the subject of differences among analysts in regard to their use of theory is an important topic, to which I return throughout this book, my aims at present are more limited. I shall describe here the general approach that I have adopted in applying psychoanalytic theory to psychoanalytic technique. In this approach the free association method is the central point of reference. Initial formulation of clinical events from the viewpoint of the free association method provides a useful articulation with the multidimensional propositions of psychoanalytic theory. It emphasizes the interpretation of the observational data in terms of the method used to obtain them. While this is generally the way all analysts do their work, I believe that I make use of the free association method in a more operational fashion than is commonly expressed in psychoanalytic writings. This approach offers a means for conceptualizing both the patient's and the analyst's participation in the psychoanalytic process. In regard to the latter it highlights the influence of the analyst's formulations on his interventions and, consequently, on the patient's free associations.

To make use of the free association method in this way of formulating clinical events, one must be able to state diagnostic assessments in similar terms and to have a corresponding conception of the nature of psychoanalytic treatment. For example, concerning treatment, I am apt to show my patients that their associations come to an unsatisfying halt, or that they miscarry, or that ordinary language breaks off and symptoms continue the expression of the patient's associations. Completion of one's associations, including thought, feeling, wish, image, sensation, and memory, leads to a sense of satisfaction, while interruption or diversion leads to a sense of dissatisfaction. Various forms of dissatisfaction result from interference with the expression of the associations, and a variety of interferences and diversions can be described. It follows that psychoanalytic treatment should aid the patient in completing the expression of his associations by helping him recognize and mas-

ter the interferences and diversions. This is one way I characterize psychoanalysis to my patients.

I find it useful to define the free association method, the
principal method of psychoanalysis, as a joint venture in
which the patient attempts to express whatever comes to mind,
that is, the free associations, and the analyst, guided by his own
associations and formulations, contributes only with the goal
of enhancing the expression of the patient's free associations.
The complex and extraordinary consequence of this mutual activity is the free association process.

This definition of the free association method may at first
seem restrictive or simplistic, for analysts generally regard free
association as only one of several sources of "material" for the
work of producing analytic understanding (e.g., Freud, 1940, p.
177). My aim in this book is to demonstrate the merits of viewing other sources of understanding, such as the transference
reactions, as the consequence of using the free association
method. For purposes of exposition I shall refer to "the analyst," to his functions, and to his responsibilities. I shall not
always repeat my firm belief that this is one way rather than the
way to practice psychoanalysis. I am always interested, however, to know why and how each analyst finds particular approaches to his taste.

The definition deliberately describes the analyst's goal in
the use of the free association method as the enhancement of
the patient's free associations and not as the production of insight, nor as the development of a regressive transference neurosis and its resolution, nor as the reduction of symptoms or
suffering. Naturally, the free association method itself is under-
taken with the therapeutic aim of reducing a broad range of
symptoms and suffering, but within the method, so to speak,
the analyst's goal is to further the process that results from
using the method. The production of insight and the development and resolution of the regressive transference neurosis are
essential components of that process, but, within the method,
insight and the vicissitudes of the transference neurosis are
subsidiary to enhancement of the patient's free associations. In
making interpretations the analyst aims to facilitate the free
association process, which is in turn expected to have an effect
upon symptoms and suffering.

To view the analyst's task in such a perspective does not contradict an alternative view that interpretations produce insight, which in turn exerts an influence upon symptoms. It is probably more accurate to say that the free association method leads concomitantly to insight, resolution of symptoms, and other aspects of the free association process. These three terms refer to overlapping descriptions of behavior and experience. For the practical purpose of outlining a formulation of psychoanalytic technique in general, I find it sufficient to recognize that they are parallel consequences of the free association method.

Similarly, it is essential to be able to formulate symptoms in terms of the free associations and the free association process for such a point of view of the analyst's function to be meaningful. I do not intend to imply that psychopathology should be equated with a disorder of free association. But I do want to emphasize: psychoanalysis has demonstrated that the components of psychopathology invariably include significant limitations in freedom of association. In this sense, Freud spoke of Fräulein Elisabeth von R.'s knowing and not knowing her loving feelings for her brother-in-law, which "were cut off from any free associative connection of thought with the rest of the ideational content of her mind" (Breuer and Freud, 1893–95, p. 165). The psychoanalytic treatment method offers a substantial approach to the resolution of psychopathology by focusing upon the limitations and disorders of free association. Its therapeutic aim is to increase the patient's freedom of association. In this book I consider the relationship between psychopathology and free association from several directions, in order to clarify the approach I am describing.

Like any other approach to formulating psychoanalytic experience, the one I have been outlining could enslave the human discourse of psychoanalysis in rigid codification. For me, it is a useful tool that helps me understand and influence my patients without interfering. It is fundamental that the associations belong to the patient. They are derivatively a part of himself, especially of his body, as they come to express feelings, needs, and desires, and as they represent his self-image, symbolically. The analyst must take care not to dispossess the patient of them. They reflect not only the patient's investment in his body but his detachment from it as well. Where the patient can be helped to possess his associations more, by understanding more of his own meaning, he regains lost connections with his body and between constituent elements of his mind.

Allusive statements such as these are, of course, relatively easy to make with any of a number of approaches to understanding patients. What appeals to me about the approach I am describing is that it permits convincing attention to clinical detail as it generates experience-near hypotheses (Waelder, 1962) about the associations. These hypotheses can then, in turn, be viewed in the perspective of one or another of the frames of reference of psychoanalytic theory at a number of levels of abstraction.

This brings me back, for a moment, to the role of theory and the differences among analysts in the use of theory. What may be crucially important in formulating the analytic process for one analyst may seem relatively unimportant to another. Furthermore, each may be different with different patients. On the other hand, I believe that a central interest in the free associations and their meaning to the patient is characteristic of all psychoanalytic treatment, of psychoanalysis proper and of its derivative therapies. Differences among analysts come into play as the selection process begins. Which elements of the associations does one put together, and how does one express the combination? Surely there is more than anyone can grasp. Valid differences in observation and selection, based on styles and interests of the analysts, not on their relative acuity or obtuseness or on their pathology, contribute to differences of theoretical emphasis. Affinity for a particular aspect of theory exerts a corresponding influence on observation and selection of free associations for clarification and interpretation. From the wide range of psychoanalytic statements and propositions, the analyst selects one or several suitable to the occasion. An individual is bound by his own predilections, however, trainable for breadth but not unlimited in scope.

Not all theoretical differences represent equally valid alternatives, nor are all selections from the free associations equally correct (where "correct" is defined as enhancing the free association process). Nor am I suggesting that theoretically or clinically "anything goes" just because some aspect of the free associations can be shown to relate to it. In a world of pro-liferating psychological highways many roads, but certainly not all of them, will lead to Rome. This book will not concern itself with theoretical differences of that sort.

The kind of valid differences I mean may be illustrated by an example. A patient in analysis is critical of my silence. His associations falter. A familiar pattern of his impatience and de-mand for attention is before us. A comment on the possible sources of his impatience or a reminder of many past situations of similar impatience that have been mentioned in recent ses-sions might well assist his further free associations. I notice, however, that his criticism of my technique has not only an impatient but a didactic sound. Two days ago he gave me ad-vice on another, entirely different matter, and his embarrass-ment about doing so was prominent in the hour between. I draw his attention to this line of continuity.

The psychoanalytic method is geared, first of all, to iden-tify continuities. As a method of observation it is radically dif-ferent from other methods of observation that tend to record and emphasize discontinuities. These continuities are, in the first place, those of thought, wish, feeling, sensation, image, and memory as they appear in the free associations, but they extend in many dimensions. In the example that I have just given, I have suggested two alternative lines of continuity. In the first, the continuity of impatience and demand is high-lighted; in the second, didactic criticism is emphasized. In the first, one might formulate a wish for the analyst to do some-thing to or for the patient, while in the second one is more apt to see that the patient wants to do something to the analyst. In an entirely different line, neither contradictory nor requisite to the other two, one may approach the present in terms of a dis-tant-past connection, or one may be drawn to events in the two most recent sessions, with or without an understanding of con-nections to the distant past. On still another plane, one may choose to emphasize, in either line, that the patient's criticism is the expression of a transference, the reactivation of a past relationship; or one may tend to emphasize the inherent ele-ments of style and wish, without reference to particular rela-tionships in which they may have been important. No one would argue against the proposition that elements of interpretation and clarification such as these would generally be suitable, individually or in combination, depending upon the circumstances of the clinical event, here presented only in the barest outline. The point that I should like to emphasize, however, is that the continuities chosen by the analyst for intervention and the perspectives in which he sees them, the formulations that guide his interventions, depend not only upon the patient but upon the analyst as well.

I make such a point of the differences among analysts in order to highlight those features of the psychoanalytic process that we hold in common. For me, the central point in psychoanalysis is the commitment to the free association method, as I have already indicated. I intend, now, to examine some features of the method and of the process that results from its use. In doing so I shall attempt to create a composite picture by selecting for discussion a series of individual clinical matters and their relationship to free association.

2

Varieties of Free Association

It may be clear already that I use the term *free association* in a number of different ways. It is, first of all, a sequence of thoughts, feelings, wishes, sensations, and images, present or remembered, expressed from a variety of perspectives. The sequential quality, relatively unencumbered by consciously directed, purposeful organization, characterizes free association in this sense. Such sequences of mental activity are the ordinary stuff of everyday life (Lewin, 1955, pp. 274−81). Here is a brief example.

One day, when the question of whether to become an analyst was still before me, as I was headed out to do some spring gardening, I found myself wondering about psychoanalysis and what could possibly be the good of a treatment that only uses words. I did not take the question particularly seriously and, so I thought, forgot it entirely. Sometime later, perhaps fifteen minutes, I found myself recalling these familiar lines from "Daffodils":

For oft when on my couch I lie,
In vacant or in pensive mood,
They flash upon that inward eye,
Which is the bliss of solitude;

I became aware that I had returned to my original topic, more or less. I was pleased to see that in the poet's name, Wordsworth, I found my original question, and I took the whole sequence as something of a positive answer.

The sequence of thoughts, feelings, images, and memories I think of as "the free associations," or "the associations." In this example, the associations include not only the explicit elements but also the form in which I expressed doubt and affirmation, wanting and not wanting to pay attention to the question on my mind. The activity that produces the sequence is "free association."[1] The "method of free association," involving two people, attempts to employ this activity in the analytic situation. Extended use of the method leads to the "free association process."

In all these terms, the word "free" connotes the absence of conscious direction. In speaking of "freedom of association" or "freedom of free association," however, I refer to the absence of unconscious restrictions (resistances). For example, I am apt to assess freedom of association as an important measure of clinical condition, especially as a measure of progress in treatment.

Intimately connected with these terms is the implicit assumption of unconscious or preconscious determinants as *organizing principles* of the associations that contribute a significant aspect of meaning. For me, the process of free association yields a necessary enrichment of conscious meaning for the patient. This is one aspect of insight.

When I speak of varieties of free association, it is as a psychoanalytic clinician, referring to differences of form, quality, or function of the associations, in the free association process. This chapter will focus mainly on form, style, and modality of expression, while the next one will be devoted more to functions of free association. I shall begin with two examples in which the free association is influenced by a single major determinant.

There is a common and important kind of analytic session that can be characterized by the mutual conclusion of patient and analyst: "Now I understand what happened yesterday." Sometimes the patient may know at the start that there was a problem in some event of the previous day. Often there is only vague uneasiness that focuses on a particular matter in the course of the hour. The substance of the hour leads to the formulation of the source of this uneasiness in the experience of the day before. For instance, in the analysis of a young man, the associations, including a dream, clearly referred to a masturbatory experiment of the day before. I inferred that the patient

---

1. It is merely a matter of linguistic preference that I omit the participle of an imaginary verb, "to free associate."

must have been afraid that he had injured his penis. When I asked, he recalled such a fear and experienced relief of uneasiness.

Another instance of a similar kind of hour reached a little deeper. A man was furious with his wife for having bought tickets for a baseball game for the wrong day. His associations led us back to a time when he was a boy of ten, ill and confined to bed. Radio broadcasts of the baseball games had given him an essential avenue for hope that he might grow up to be a man. The associations brought together for him a number of valuable connections: from observation of excessive anger; to memory of the particular importance of baseball; to an awareness that his fury at his wife was a response to revived past helplessness, with fears of death and of injury.

In these two examples, the free associations can be readily construed as serving the analytic purpose. They are the tools with which patient and analyst help the patient to complete the expression of thoughts and feelings—in this case from the day before. In the second example the link to a frightening past experience that had significantly injured his already precarious self-esteem alerted the patient to chronic interruptions in his thoughts and feelings in a new way.

These hours belong to a subgroup of the class in which the free associations are determined predominantly by one main source. Examples of other subgroups in this class include hours following dreams or hours preceding important life events or separations in the analysis.

This way of classifying the varieties of free association takes note of their effective organizing principles. They may be, as in the examples, a question that is barely out of conscious awareness, a long forgotten fear, or the flame of an old personal injury rekindled in the course of analysis by a minor frustration. At other times an internal conflict determines the associations, first from one side, then from the other. Or the organizing influence may lie in a memory of a relationship emerging in the free association process as a transference. Enduring traits of character also determine the form of the free associations, sometimes revealing particular disorders of development (e.g., A. Kris, 1979). Much of the time, however, the psychoanalytic hour does not yield a sharply definable single determinant. In such hours one can delineate, nonetheless, a number of trends at work determining the free associations. One of the ordinary tensions in the analytic process is the conflict between a focus on one main determinant of the associations or several operating at once. The resolution of such a conflict in any particular hour will be the product of two minds at work.

Although the two hours I described display a condition of benevolent cooperation between patient and analyst, with transference not prominent at all, similar hours may occur in the context of intense transference reactions. Some particular event that catches the patient's affective attention becomes the chief determinant of the free associations in these hours, whatever transference conditions may prevail within the analysis.

Here is a somewhat extreme example, both in the intensity of the transference reaction and the intercurrent event. A young man in the second year of analysis became increasingly querulous and anxious. He interrupted himself incessantly. Any hint of his feeling relaxed and speaking freely brought him to another hostile question or complaint about the analysis. Several years later I could have helped him by spelling out the various components of his fears from a number of developmental experiences, in relation to both parents, but especially his father. At that time, however, I was still mainly ignorant of the origins of this transference reaction. What little I could say gave him small comfort. There seemed to be a significant possibility that he would not tolerate the analytic procedure or this analyst at any rate.

He called me between sessions to say that a favorite uncle had died unexpectedly. The analytic relationship reverted to its previously benign and friendly, cooperative spirit, and the frightened, hostile transference disappeared for the moment. The associations were concerned with loss, mourning, and reminiscence. Love for the lost uncle flowed in my direction, and the associations linked us as helpful supporters of the patient, in contrast to his parents. The negative transference returned not long thereafter, but it never again threatened to disrupt the treatment, though it reached an intensity among the greatest I have encountered.

The free associations and external events are not always so obliging as in these three examples. They do not always clarify or bring the obscure to light. In whose analysis have the associations not been parceled out for purposes of receiving admiration, or for revenge, or for an oppositional effect? Which analyst has not had the experience of correctly understanding his patient's transference hostility only to hear his attempts to make the patient aware of it fall victim to a fierce dissection of the analyst's words, allegedly in the service of further understanding? At such moments the form of association, the way the patient uses language, rather than the content, conveys the meaning.

Nor, of course, are the free associations confined to the verbal sphere (Kanzer, 1958, 1961). The ordinary transactions of schedule and fee, entrance and exit, position and movement on the couch, appearance, dress, the placement of a coat or pocketbook, the tone of voice, the pace of association, and many more are ready vehicles for their expression. The verbal sphere, too, is subject to any number of variations of form that may carry the meaning. Within a single hour the patient may speak or be silent, may report on recent events outside the analysis, may recall past experience, may question, may lecture, may express thoughts or affects, and so on. All these, it seems to me, are properly regarded as varieties of free association.

Classified in this way there is a large but not infinite variety of free associations for any one patient. Some highly characteristic forms develop and become part of the shorthand of communication between patient and analyst. That is not to say, however, that new forms may not emerge or be developed in the course of analysis. To take a common example, there are patients who treat their dreams concretely as private experience at the beginning of analysis. They may report them in detail, but they cannot or will not permit the elucidation of dream meaning. As the analysis proceeds, however, on other fronts, their dreams may fully enter the free association process.

While the patient is one determiner of the varieties of free association, the analyst is another. To return to an earlier theme, one way of formulating differences among analysts is according to the varieties of free association that speak to them most clearly. In the course of analysis, the analyst's proclivities of this sort are bound to influence the patient's choice of associative form.

It is possible, of course, to make classifications of the many varieties of free association according to any number of organizing principles. These may encompass smaller or greater portions of time, from parts of one hour to sequences of hours or periods of many weeks or months. The longer the segment of analysis, the more a variety of free association becomes a pattern in the free association process. Such classifications represent one kind of theoretical formulation employed, more or less explicitly, by the analyst.

I shall not attempt here to delineate further classifications or to create a typology of free associations. On the contrary, I want to emphasize the analyst's need to formulate classifications in the analytic situation as the occasion arises. I have tried to illustrate my use of terms and to demonstrate some of the multiple aspects and many varieties of free association. I have not attempted to discuss how the analyst or even this analyst makes his selections and formulations. That important topic lies outside the scope of this book.

3

Functions of Free Association

Psychoanalysis does not create free association in the treatment setting. It merely provides an alteration in the conditions of ordinary association toward freedom from conscious direction. It shifts the balance of attention from outward to inward, it replaces silent soliloquy with spoken words, and it establishes a human relationship whose aims are confined to promoting the patient's free associations in the service of a therapeutic objective.

Viewed in this way, psychoanalysis must appear an improbable venture to any but those who have experienced the powerful effects of the measures described. In this chapter I shall attempt to delineate some of the many functions of the free association method that lead to those effects.

When I speak of functions I refer to a number of overlapping formulations of free association in terms of the effects produced. From the point of view of psychoanalysis as a technique or as a therapeutic modality, these effects are purposes, under the general heading of increased freedom of association. In this sense it is the aim of free association to make conscious what is unconscious, to recall what is forgotten, to regain lost experience, to complete mourning, to elucidate inner conflict, to expand what is condensed, to put thought and feeling into words, to clarify confusion, and to reverse disorientation. Any one of these and many more may serve as the organizing principle for classifying the free associations.

I find it useful to emphasize one aspect of all these functions: the promotion of continuity. I have in mind the continuity of expression, thought, affect, sensation, memory, sense of self, personal history, relationship to the environment, and so on. When I mentioned the formulation of psychopathology from the viewpoint of free association in chapter 1, I was referring to discontinuities in these spheres, demonstrable by the method of free association. Discontinuities of this sort are limitations or disorders of freedom of association.

The two examples, given in the last chapter, of hours dominated by a disturbing event of the day before demonstrate a number of these functions. In the second example, unconscious memories of fears and narcissistic injury connected with the patient's childhood illness were revived by his wife's error about the baseball tickets. They were brought to conscious awareness in the course of free association the following day, in words and feeling. In this way he regained lost experience, for though he had remembered the illness, he had forgotten his feelings. He clarified a confusing reaction of the day before, and he enhanced his orientation to himself and to his wife.

It may be worth noting that in this instance the elucidation of conflict was not prominent. That is, we learned little directly on this occasion concerning the reasons for his having to repress the fears and narcissistic injury. We guessed correctly that the fury at his wife was one example among many of old anger at his mother, and that this rage dated not only to the illness at age ten, when he overheard her say that the doctor had thought he might not recover his strength or might even die, but also to earlier injuries. But a guess, no matter how right, whether it is made by the patient or by the analyst, is very far from having the force of free association. We had to settle for renewed evidence of his chronic ambivalence to his wife—conflict between feelings of love and resentment—not much clarified.

The example of the young man who was afraid that he had injured his penis had a somewhat different quality. This young man, whose early childless marriage had ended most unhappily in divorce, was sexually very active, both with women partners and in masturbation. He felt very inadequate on account of what he regarded as his virtually insatiable sexuality and on account of his personal and social failures. Masturbation was always a matter of ambivalence: a great source of pleasure but proof of immaturity, of being alone, and of lack of

self-control. In the distant background, far from conscious
awareness, he blamed his childhood sexuality for destroying
an early good relationship with his mother.

The hour in question occurred at the beginning of Septem-
ber. The patient had been aware the day before of being angry
with me and had himself supposed it was related to my recent
vacation absence. He began the session somewhat belligerently
and then wondered why he was in a fighting mood. He was
disappointed that I hadn't helped him put things together
about a failure with a recent girlfriend, and he went on to talk
about another woman who was limiting her involvement with
him and had left town for a weekend trip to relatives. References to his ex-wife followed. These comments culminated in
hints of loneliness, for he missed the woman who was away. He
spoke of one woman taking him from another, to his later re-
gret. He knew that he was not "the hottest thing on wheels," he
said. He tried to reassure himself by emphasizing his attractive-
ness, noting that several women had wanted him, reminding
himself that he had rejected certain women, and stating that he
felt more confident and less insecure than he had earlier. His
improvement, however, had been due not to the analytic work
but to the relationship with the particular woman he had been
involved with, he added. The flow of words faltered; he talked
about feeling depressed and said something about his feelings
getting in his way. At this point he called for help. "Can you
say something?" I asked him what he had in mind. He wondered if I could confirm or deny what he said, and he added
that he felt he was running out of gas in the session.

I said that it seemed that he missed me, too. Dissatisfied, he
replied that I wasn't there to be silent. He went on to report a
failure at work. Then came a failure with another woman, who
was not attractive enough. His thoughts returned to his present
woman friend, and he said he wanted her to blow him. Then he
remembered that he had had a dream last night. He wasn't sure
if this one had woken him up, or another one. As a preamble he
told me that he was having two types of trouble with his car—a
door handle had come off and the car leaked in the rain.

I was in my car, which I had to park in a slum area. I tried to
drive it out, but I couldn't. When I came back, I found the

top dented in and the car burned and charred, but it was not destroyed. I called my father to pick me up.

He was anxious about his car, he said, and then he linked past dreams about cars with breakups with other women, especially with his divorce. He said he was masturbating more freely and frequently now and went on to speak of how many times a day he needed to have an orgasm. With his girlfriend he had had three orgasms. Alone, he had masturbated twice and had felt better. Two or three times a day, he said, was best for him. He thought of a government official he had encountered as part of his job who was not as friendly as he would have liked; and then, after a pause, he said, "Part of me gets angry when you don't respond to my requests." I said that it wasn't clear what his request was for. He replied that he was lonely. In the dream he calls his father, I noted. Yes, he said, but why did I mention that? What did it have to do with the difficulty here? "What difficulty?" I asked. He couldn't answer; he didn't know. I offered a guess: the masturbation, the slum area. He criticized my Freudian bias, typical of a psychiatrist, but then a moment later he acknowledged feeling a little uncomfortable about it. He had tried to mimic his former girlfriend's pleasurably nibbling his penis. He wondered if it was a perversion. He had twisted a pipe cleaner around his penis, and it gave him a similar feeling. At this point I asked him whether he had feared hurting himself, whether he had cut himself or scratched himself. He had scratched himself, he replied, relieved and somewhat surprised that I had guessed it. I pointed out that he had expressed that fear in the dream, beginning with the phrase, "When I came." The car was damaged but not destroyed. (I also had in mind the repeated pairing in two kinds of car trouble, two dreams, and masturbating twice, in which he linked himself with the car. In the expressions "not the hottest thing on wheels" and "running out of gas" he had identified himself with a car, but I was not consciously aware of those references at this moment.) I said it seemed that having been afraid, he had wanted to ask me whether it was all right. I suggested that it was probably an old fear. He now recalled that he had had to ejaculate very forcibly and felt it was like a top shooting off.

The conflict between remembering and repressing the frightening experience of masturbating the day before provided an opportunity to observe the intense self-criticism in operation. He wished to talk about his fear and his injury, but he felt he had caused his own troubles and deserved no help. Plainly, not far from the surface, the fear was equated with castration and rejection as proper punishment.

While I can imagine any number of possible interventions, it is not all that easy in advance to know how to thread one's way among the conflicting forces. I chose the safety of pointing out a missing association, the fear he had forgotten, which brought relief. The most superficial conflict at present was between expression and repression, and it proved sufficient to expose that in order to promote the free association process. No matter how one may formulate such an event, it would be hard to overlook the contrast between self-punitive repression and the freedom of thought and feeling gained from free association in this analytic experience.

The patient was quite correct in his observation that car dreams bore a relationship to breakups of relationships with women. A little over a year later in the analysis of the same patient, a remarkably similar occurrence gave us a chance to proceed with aspects of themes left unexplored in the hour just described. It took place a few days before he was to visit his mother at her home, in a foreign country. This second hour followed the recent termination of a relationship with a woman he loved. He had been most critical of himself in the previous session for wanting someone, clearly his analyst, to take care of him in her place. He was certain that I, too, would be critical of these wishes. He began this Monday session with a dream.

> I am in a foreign country. I had been driving. I had parked my car. I wondered if it might rain. I wanted to go back to the place I parked it to close the windows. I asked a guy where my car was parked and he said, "At O."

Someone had broken the light fixture on his car on Saturday, he said. He mentioned again several women with whom he had been involved at various times. One of them had said that he didn't seem able to be involved with anyone at present.

Another, whom he had been with on Saturday night, just didn't turn him on, and he didn't want to spend the night. Nobody had called. Was he a victim of his past or was it still continuing this way? He felt he was loud and coarse. It had been a bad weekend, although he did feel more equal with his male friends now. He was afraid of getting depressed, spending so much time on the lousy stuff in his life. He hadn't been in love with anyone in a long time, he said. He felt he was adjusting to a solipsistic existence, getting numb.

On Saturday night he had parked in a loading zone. That was the zero in the dream, he felt: he paid nothing to park. The parking lot would have cost him a dollar. Everything was boring to him, including this session. He had recognized a woman whom he had known in college and had dated for two weeks. It had been torrid, but he couldn't be with her; she was not for him. He has decided not to sleep with somebody he doesn't like, feeling it would be dishonest, using someone. After a few more comments on the lack of pleasure in his life he explained to me that I was glimpsing the experience of his whole weekend. I agreed. He said he wasn't depressed now—only mildly so, in any case. He felt that he got more out of analysis when he was with people. At present he has no close friends of his own age. He felt stuck. "I make a hit over fifty and under ten." I suggested that perhaps that was the zero of the dream: "You get nothing." "Almost nothing," he said, "my job is going well." And then he began to list a few good friends. After a moment or two, however, he noted again that it was a boring hour. At least he wasn't decidedly depressed, he said. But he felt he was up to nothing. He felt he should write a story: "Up to Nothing." To my ear this sounded like "up to no good"; so I said, "You keep coming back to masturbation and to nothing." He said he masturbated in all three nights of the weekend, and it bothered him. "Was there something different about the masturbation?" I asked. "One thing," he said. On Sunday he had wrapped the bathrobe belt around his testicles to simulate a woman playing with him. I referred to *The Story of O*. He had never read it, but he knew it was about sex and a woman. "Perversion," I said. Yes, he knew that. I suggested that that was what he was saying about himself. He then added that he thought sometimes of some masochistic perverse experiences, such as he had read in Genet, being tied up and whipped. "That's what I'm left to." I suggested that we needed to know more about it.

In fact, we heard little more about perverse fantasies in the subsequent years of analysis, and so far as I could tell they were not a major component of his fantasy life. His mood changed for the better, however, and, incidentally, we learned the next day that the bathrobe came from his mother. The most prominent association, to my ear, in this hour was the boredom. Very frequently such boredom refers, as it did here, to the consequences of repression. Applied to the dream, the associations referred to his wish to regain feeling; they also referred to a wish to return to the place of excitement, at nothing, which to me meant his mother's genitals. Interpolated within that sequence, however, was the story that he wanted to write. That led me to the topics of masturbation and perversion and the possibility that some specific, exciting experience was being kept out of the hour. The self-criticism for his "perverse" fantasies and actions appears to have been uppermost in his mind at this moment. That is, lonely, away from me, he feared his desire to return to mother, both out of loneliness and out of sexual desire. Perhaps the two-week torrid relationship he spoke of is a reference to unconscious fantasies connected with the visit home.

From the point of view of functions of free association, the second hour permitted the patient to regain the excited and alive involvement with his own body and to want a woman to be interested in it. The experience of boredom within the session resulted from inhibition of this wish. Furthermore, the discontinuity produced by the conflicts between wish and self-criticism was reversed. Where the first hour had placed an emphasis upon anxiety, the second brought self-criticism more clearly into conscious awareness. In each case the session was representative of the period of analysis in which it occurred. Both sessions could also be seen as steps toward the reconstruction of a continuity of personal experience in loving. Love for mother early in life and for other women in his adult life was bound up in painful and depressing conflicts in all instances.

In my view, the concept of perversion adds little to the

understanding of the two experiences described. Rather, I think more is to be gained by considering these two sexual experiments as attempts to incorporate the wish for a partner into the masturbatory experience. (This may well have been represented by the pairs that appeared in the associations of the first dream session.) The patient's emphasis tends to the concrete, responding, I believe, to a greater than average real loss of mother in the early oedipal phase of development. These two isolated instances and the subsequent hours can be viewed as part of the process of remembering that is one of the most valuable functions of free association, especially when it leads to mourning for loss, clarification of childhood misconceptions, and revision of maladaptive solutions to conflict.

These sessions also demonstrate the effects of free association on the relationship between patient and analyst. In both instances, the patient was extremely satisfied by the experience of being assisted and understood. In both, there was some clarification of the transference as well, though in neither did that play a major part.

This example gives me one more opportunity to emphasize how many different approaches might be taken. Surely no one could argue with an analyst who sooner or later within the hour pointed out that the patient was in fact on his way to a foreign country, opening up a significant line of entry into the analysis of the dream. Some analysts might have been inclined, especially in the second hour, well into the analysis, to bring more elements together. They might have linked the multiple self-criticisms for wanting to be a freeloader, for masturbation, and for "perverse" incestuous fantasies with transference wishes heightened by the coming separation.

4
The Method of Free Association

The method of free association, as I have come to formulate it for myself, is a joint venture that patient and analyst undertake in the service of the patient's therapeutic goals. The patient attempts to express in words all thoughts, feelings, wishes, sensations, images, and memories without reservation. The analyst, guided by his own associations, attempts to aid the patient in this task. The complex ensuing consequences are the process of free association. In this process, the therapeutic goals are approached by promoting associative continuity and increasing freedom of association.

Just as analysts vary in their theoretical formulation of meaning in the patient's associations, they vary also in their conception of the psychoanalytic enterprise and the division of responsibilities between the two participants. In this exposition of my own approach I shall focus principally on the analyst's responsibilities. A central feature of my views is that the analyst has no rights of authority within the method of free association. By this I mean that the analyst assists the patient in the task of free association without interfering with the patient's exclusive right and responsibility to make decisions for himself. In asserting that the analyst needs no independent authority to perform this function, I am in disagreement with tradition in regard to the role of the analyst, as it derives from a still earlier model of the physician. I believe this view, however, to be in keeping with the developing aims of psychoanalytic technique as it has evolved from its origins in hypnosis. Gray (1981) has recently emphasized a similar position.

In focusing on the responsibilities of the analyst, I limit my discussion to an outline of his functions in the method and process of free association. I do not attempt to describe how the analyst performs his functions, what inner qualities he calls upon, what training he requires, or how he maintains the balance between involvement and objectivity, between conscious and unconscious influences on his own associations, and between experiencing and formulating. These important matters lie outside the scope of this book. In regard to the last of them, however, the role of formulation, I hope to facilitate new lines of inquiry and research, by describing the process of psychoanalysis in terms of the method of free association, more operationally than theoretically. I shall return to this subject in chapter 13.

The psychoanalytic concept of interpretation and of the analyst as interpreter can serve as a starting point for a discussion of the analyst's responsibilities. Later chapters will consider the scope and functions of interpretation itself. Interpretation in psychoanalysis means translation from inferred unconscious language (of symptom and dream originally) into the everyday language of conscious discourse. What of the interpreter? While the analyst is in one way like the unseen speaker whose voice transmitted electronically at an international meeting conveys a message from one language to another, unlike such translators he must exercise a selective and a synthetic function in addition. For other purposes, too, he must be fully present—in some ways, not in others. To meet his responsibilities as a participant in the free association method, the analyst learns to translate expertly from one form of expression to another. That is, when the analyst recognizes unconscious meaning in the associations, he makes use of the insight to promote the patient's further associations, to promote a process. To the extent that the analyst directs the patient to address his free associations to the analyst as expert, however (or accepts the patient's wish to do so as realistic), he assumes unwarranted and unnecessary authority. He is neither Joseph, plenipotentiary, nor wise and selfless sibyl.

At this juncture, the concept of the analyst's anonymity intersects usefully with this consideration of the analyst as interpreter. Anonymity means more than that the analyst should keep his personal affairs to himself—though that is essential, not out of slavish devotion to secrecy but out of respect for the patient's exclusive proprietary rights in the free association method. In my description of analysis to prospective patients and in the form of my interventions in the course of analysis, I emphasize that it is the method of free association, with the analyst as a participant, rather than the analyst as an individual, that is the source of analytic knowledge. As I understand it, the analyst should remain anonymous except as a participant in the method. The analyst as authoritative expert, however, far from anonymous, is an extraneous presence.[1] On the other hand, the patient's free associations may well designate the analyst as an expert. Clarification of such an attitude requires further expansion through free association. The analyst neither accepts it nor rejects it—that would be the unwarranted exercise of authority, of proprietary rights. The analyst must assess the relationship of such an attitude to the process of free association. Sooner or later the promotion of the process of free association may require some intervention on the analyst's part in regard to the significance and meanings of such an attitude.

The designation of the analyst as expert may be essential for some patients for a time. It may, for example, be necessary as part of an idealization of the analyst (Kohut, 1966; Spruiell, 1979). To the extent that the free associations proceed, no intervention by the analyst is required. When idealization proves to interfere with free association, the analyst may have to help the patient recognize (or, as we say loosely, "analyze") an apparent conflict between idealization and other interests—for example, wishes to be independent or to denigrate the analyst.

All patients at times need to denigrate their analysts. One common way is to devalue any intervention the analyst may make, starting with the quality of greeting at the door. The analyst under these circumstances does not withdraw from participation and give an expert opinion; he aims whatever interventions he may make toward expansion of the patient's hostile thoughts and feelings. His efforts depend, ultimately, on the patient's preference for the method of free association over the

---

1. I am aware that, at times, exceptions to this rule are necessary. For example, parents in analysis may need guidance in regard to their children that cannot always be postponed until the process of analysis comes to the matter in question (A. Kris, 1981).

satisfactions of denigrating the analyst. This preference is one measure of therapeutic alliance (Greenson, 1967; Zetzel, 1971, chap. 11).

I want to take up one more valuable term used to describe the responsibilities of the analyst, the concept of neutrality. This does not refer to a personal indifference or unfriendliness on the analyst's part. On the contrary, the analyst is biased in his patient's favor, allied with the patient in the pursuit of the patient's goals, and as tactful as possible in making interventions (Stone, 1961). When Freud recommended that analysts operate like surgeons, it did not mean that he regarded surgeons as callous. He meant, clearly, that the surgeon has no right to be squeamish when he holds the scalpel in his hand. The analyst, likewise, compensated for his time, must sacrifice personal preference, whether harsh or tender. He does not choose the topic; he must not favor one side of a patient's conflict over the other; nor can he claim exemption from the emotional demands made upon him in the process of free association. These are proprietary rights in ordinary human relations that the analyst relinquishes in his professional role.

Some may object at this point. Does the analyst not decide on his own schedule and on his fees? Does the analyst not decide when to intervene and how?

True, the analyst makes the decision, for himself, whether to enter the partnership, and, within limits, he is entitled to compensation and to set a schedule. Once the decision has been made, however, the analyst's actions are determined by the patient's needs, principally by the patient's free associations. When it comes to timing, however, a different sort of answer is called for. The view that the analyst has some insight waiting to be "given" to the patient appears to me to be illusion. It is easy enough to see far ahead in analysis. To know what is needed at a particular moment, however, to permit some small, often barely noticeable expansion of the freedom of association is the difficult fundamental task of the psychoanalyst. To see a mountain peak in the distance is very different from making the arduous journey over uncharted terrain. Analysis follows the path of the free associations—affected by the interventions of the analyst, but necessarily also affecting the analyst who makes them. Like any assumption of authority by the analyst, introduction of his own tempos tends to impose an interference with the method that may obscure the road we seek to travel.

Nothing I have said is intended to convey the impression that I see the analyst as a silent partner. Silence or speaking on the part of the analyst serves to foster free association. Neither holds any significance beyond this aim. Nor do I picture the analyst as either active or passive. Analyst and patient are both active and passive. Patients often begin the analysis with a view of the analyst as active and themselves as passive—at least, that is the surface impression. And sooner or later in most analyses the patient experiences the relationship as "unfair," in the sense that the patient must reveal all but expect no return in kind and must love unrequited. Clarification and interpretation of such transference reactions will be most readily assimilated by the patient—with corresponding progress in the freedom of association—if the patient can recognize the reality of the analyst's intentions and obligations. That is, the analyst responds only when he has something useful to say. He must not yield to the temptations of responding to love and hate in any way except to promote free association, and he must remember that he is paid for attending to the patient's associations, with no right to talk about himself for his own purposes or satisfaction.

These thoughts add another dimension to the advantages of formulating the psychoanalytic treatment process in terms of a method of free association. The view of two participants with distinct functions serves not only to clarify the terms of therapeutic alliance in the joint purpose of fostering the patient's free associations and to diminish certain common errors of unintentional authoritarianism. It also provides a reliable backdrop for the dramatic action of the transference.

I want to illustrate some of these matters with the common problem of the patient's questions. Questions arise out of many reasons, for many purposes, but they are always part of the free association method. A patient who had had an earlier, beneficial analysis with another analyst asks a question and then adds, "I won't get an answer." My response is: "You will get a reply, but I don't have the answer." Implied was the reminder: "By externalization you seek to make an inner conflict over proceeding with your associations adversarial, and you expect rejection when you feel in need of help." Both had many times been clarified before. He acknowledged at once that he knew I often reply to such questions and continued on his way.

Frequently patients ask personal questions about the analyst, though hardly ever intimately personal ones. They usually ask questions whose answers are generally known in the community or can be found in directories. My position is that if, on sufficient reflection, the patient decides that he really wants the answer, then I will answer, and I do. One such instance occurred in the analysis of a man who attended the same college as I did, but who had not known me there. He wanted to know where I went to college. He had a fantasy of my having gone to what he regarded as an inferior school, as part of a powerful need to denigrate me. To tell him the answer risked interfering with a vitally important transference. I said I would answer, but I suggested that he take his time about deciding if he wanted the answer. Several years later, when this transference had been well analyzed, he sat up suddenly in the middle of an hour with a broad grin on his face. He had looked me up in the library. This is a little longer than it usually takes patients to decide on whether they want the answer. In my opinion, in this instance, his timing was sound.

Several patients have at times tried to use questions in the way that a point of order may be introduced under Robert's Rules. Such "technical" questions are intended by the patient to supersede the psychoanalytic method, to have a privileged status. Mostly such questions reflect the patient's sense of overwhelming tension in the heat of the analytic moment. Acknowledgment of a need to withdraw from that tension proves helpful, often permitting immediate return to free association.

The analyst, in my view, is not the arbiter among the patient's conflicting needs, wishes, and intentions. If the patient expresses the wish or if the patient acts on the wish to avoid free association or to miss analytic sessions, it is not the analyst's function to judge, to approve, or to disapprove. It is the analyst's function to assist the patient in putting into words the conflicting tendencies at work—those in the direction of continuing free association and those opposed. I find it useful in these kinds of conflicts to borrow from Dr. Johnson's advice to authors: "that men more frequently require to be reminded than informed" (1750, p. 14).

There are, it is true, some occasions when an analyst must assist a patient to become aware of danger. As I have come to be clearer about my aims in these rare instances, I have found that the main thrust is always one of helping the patient recognize a powerful self-critical tendency that interferes with expression of some cherished loves or hates. Here the neutrality of the analyst can be stated in another way: he must empathize with the several and conflicting desires and ambitions that characterize any person's ordinary state of affairs and which the analytic process is apt to intensify at times. An example of a patient's acting out his fantasies may be helpful.

During the summer vacation, a young business man who usually operated successfully and prudently in financial matters had been approached by a representative of a large brokerage firm, who appealed to his vanity. He began, quite imprudently, to invest a significant sum, giving the unknown and even unseen broker a virtually free hand to speculate. It was clear that the patient's actions were not consonant with his usual practice. It was soon also clear that he and the broker were, from his point of view, unconsciously in collusion against the paternal authority of the absent analyst. Unfortunately, there also was a powerful self-destructive element, based on guilt toward his father. The patient recognized readily that I was right in my views of his imprudence, which I based explicitly on his usual practices and standards, not on some independent judgment of my own about the quality of the investments or the future of the stock market. Nonetheless, although he gained considerable understanding of his motives, thoughts, and feelings in this dangerous action, it took several weeks before he could act on my warnings.

The responsibility of the analyst to warn patients of impending dangers is based not upon the authority of the analyst or upon some superior understanding of the world. It derives from the analyst's functions in the free association method. Although both participants are emotionally involved in the process, the analyst's part does not lead to the loss of perspective and imbalance of motivations and restraints that are to some extent the inevitable temporary fate of the patient. This difference in analyst and patient also contributes to their everyday participation in the free association method. The analyst's relatively greater vigilance, in addition to his training and experience, makes it more his responsibility to assess the course and meanings of the associations. The determination of when and how to conclude the treatment is an instance of the latter, though the final decision in that judgment, I believe, should be left to the patient (Ticho, 1972). Where the analyst must decide unilaterally, owing to some disorder of the patient's capacity to exercise his own judgment, the limits of applicability of the free association method have already been breached.

The arrangements of fee and schedule provide a point of special importance in a consideration of the analyst's responsibilities in the free association method. At that point the analyst's self-interest and his interest in the patient's welfare may intersect, for the analyst, after all, makes his living by the hour. Analysts differ in regard to level of fee, willingness to scale fee in response to the patient's financial need, and estimation of the degree to which analysis should be permitted to exert a financial pressure upon the patient and his family. They also differ in regard to flexibility of schedule and charges for sessions missed through illness and holidays or on account of the demands of the patient's work or family obligations. Analysts seem to agree, however, on the need to inform the patient at the very beginning of the treatment of their position on these matters. Nonetheless, conflicts over scheduling and payment of fees usually play some role in every analysis. In those instances where such conflicts are prominent, the lengthy process of repeated attempts to clarify and to understand what is at stake proves to be an important part of the process of free association. The resolution of ambiguities in this area of analysis, as in others, can never be arbitrary. It is essential, I believe, to recognize that in regard to fee and schedule the analyst must exert both judgment and authority in setting forth his position. While it is necessary, ultimately, for patient and analyst to come to some agreement in terms of action, here as elsewhere it is never incumbent upon the patient to agree with the analyst's policy or judgment.

Finally, it will be clear that I do not picture the analyst as "curing" the patient or even as "analyzing" the patient. I ascribe such functions to the method of free association. To analyze, in that sense, is an intransitive verb referring to the psychoanalyst's participation in that method. Together patient and analyst may analyze a conflict, a dream, or reactions that develop in the course of analysis.

5

Reluctance, Resistance, and Negative Attitudes

Nothing is more characteristic of the free association method than the varieties of opposition that are encountered when patient and analyst set about to use it. I find it helpful to consider the forms of opposition under two headings: reluctance and resistance. In doing so, I use the term *resistance* to refer only to unconscious obstacles to freedom of association, a much narrower sense than is usual in the psychoanalytic literature, and I use *reluctance* to mean any conscious attitude of disinclination to participate in the free association method or in analysis. Although they may be bound together, their linkage is not obligatory. While a patient's emerging negative transference, for example, may be accompanied by conscious unwillingness to participate in the free association method and by an unconscious obstacle to freedom of association that obscures the origins of the negative attitude, each of the two types frequently appears alone. These two types of opposition may or may not be accompanied by negative attitudes toward the analyst and analysis, and negative attitudes may occur with or without opposition to free association.

A patient's decision to be absent from the analysis for external reasons, such as for business purposes, for vacation, or for love, represents reluctance to proceed but is not necessarily due to resistance. Reluctance frequently also develops in anticipation of pain or other frightening prospects in analysis, for example, when the free associations threaten to bring back painful memories. Such attitudes may appear without resentment or anger toward the analyst, nor need they be based primarily on the operation of unconscious influences. On the contrary, it is important that the analyst, in his position of neutrality with respect to the patient's conflicting wishes, not regard a patient's preference for a holiday, for example, as a priori evidence of a negative attitude or lack of positive motivation. (This becomes especially difficult when the patient, out of unconscious guilt, tries to provoke such an interpretation as punishment.) It is also important to distinguish between *reluctance* that occurs in conscious anticipation of intolerable affect, especially shame and humiliation, and *resistance*, which operates unconsciously. I return to this distinction in chapter 8, when I take up the management of two contrasting kinds of conflict.

Extreme reluctance may appear episodically in the course of analysis, whenever the patient expects a traumatic consequence, a narcissistic injury. For example, this may occur when the associations lead to matters for which the patient expects, consciously or unconsciously, to be criticized by the analyst. Such a reaction is often rationalized by the patient, but so far as I have been able to determine, the patient is, at first, not conscious of its sources. In these instances reluctance results from resistance, with either positive or negative attitude toward the analyst.

Narcissistic reluctance also appears from the start as a relatively enduring characteristic. It can remain concealed, in two senses. First, the patient deliberately reserves special rights to refrain from speaking of certain matters, without giving any hint of doing so. Second, the free association method may operate successfully for considerable periods without encountering the restriction imposed. In the three most prominent instances of such concealed reluctance in my practice, the free association process seems in retrospect to have developed unimpeded, with depth and intensity, and, to the extent that one can assess such a thing, at a satisfactory rate. The reluctance did not at first link up either with resistance or with conscious negative attitudes toward the analysis and was acknowledged only when it did so. That is to say, only when the patients' positive motivation for free association, combined with their wishes for a freely positive attitude to analysis and analyst, came into conflict with the narcissistic reluctance was it "necessary" to reveal the patients' original dishonesty in the agreement to undertake the free association method. This opened up new lines of free association, different in each case. With one patient this led principally to the understanding of an aloof attitude; with a second, to the exploration of an addiction to perverse sexual fantasies; and with a third, to the resolution of a significant dishonesty.

As I have tried to formulate how and when I consider a particular opposition a resistance, I have come to the relatively narrow limits indicated earlier. Starting from the perspective of what is free about free association, I regard as resistance only those obstacles to association that arise in the absence of conscious direction. Resistance for me always means unconscious opposition to freedom of association—not opposition to treatment, to cure, or to the analyst.

In this book, where my aim is to define clinical concepts from the viewpoint of the method of free association, I limit my attention to resistance as obstacle in psychoanalytic treatment. In a wider context, Freud formulated the resistances as anti-cathexes (1926, pp. 157–58) and as the keepers of mental peace in health as well as in illness (1940, pp. 165 and 178). In such formulations, theory fills the need for organizing and coordinating data from several different sources and for extrapolating beyond the data to facilitate research. In regard to the clinical situation, Freud's metapsychological formulations summarize abstractly but most succinctly several varieties of resistance and the functions they serve, which must be taken into account by the analyst in formulating his interpretations.

To say that resistance is an unconscious obstacle to freedom of association brings into focus an intrinsic uncertainty of the free association method, for we have no independent measure of the thrust of free association against which to assess the opposition to it. It is best, I think, to acknowledge at once that the analysis of resistance ranges in difficulty from the pleasant terrain of dream and symptom analysis to the sheer rock slopes of entrenched character traits and the swampland of preverbal transference. In all these situations there are three general guides to the interaction of thrust and resistance: spontaneity, intelligibility, and satisfaction. To the extent that some thoughts come unbidden, they signal freedom from conscious direction, the hallmark of free association. To the extent that the immediate organizing principle of the associations can be delineated, encroachments on its influence by resistance can be defined. To the extent that the patient does not gain satisfaction in the process of free association, the operation of a resistance, but not its nature, can be inferred. I discuss satisfaction and dissatisfaction in free association further in chapter 7, as a separate topic. Here I need only say that I refer to satisfaction in the activity of free association, not to pleasure in its contents or to the glow of a friendly transference.

At times, as in the first of the hours from the analysis of the young man whose dreams about his car were presented in chapter 3, the patient becomes consciously aware of an interference with free association. Divorced and deserted, he asks for help; he identifies with a damaged car and says, "I'm running out of gas." This is the easy realm of the "explanatory arts," as Freud (1905, p. 116) once called them. Much of analysis takes place within these boundaries, where tension is low, cooperative spirit strong, and free association provides well-defined messages that beg to be deciphered along with a multitude of clues to meaning and to resistance.

I do not mean to give the impression that even under the optimal conditions of therapeutic alliance all resistance yields readily to the interpretive approach. That is not the case. It is remarkable to see, in retrospect, how data were concealed—not only kept out of awareness but altogether excluded from the associations. For example, a graduate student had been unable to complete the writing of her dissertation. At first, she had no understanding at all how this might be the result of inner conflict, though she was not consciously opposed to finding it out, and her inhibition was working a considerable hardship on her. After a long period of analysis, when a convincing recognition of unconscious conflicts had been reached and the dissertation was completed, she happened to recall one day, with amusement, that many years earlier she had finished the first section but had managed to leave it on a bus! She was most surprised to find that she had never mentioned it before.

I shall not attempt to detail here the manifold versions of resistance. The varieties of resistance, like the varieties of free association, can be formulated according to individual preference and the conditions of the moment. It is one of the analyst's most important interpretive functions to grasp both an emerging principle of organization of the free associations and a principle of encroachment upon them.

One way of categorizing the evidence for these encroachments is according to their mode of expression. When the associations show us both sides of an unconscious conflict, in alternation, the failure to resolve the conflict and the patient's inability to complete his thoughts about it are evidence of resistance. Similarly, partial expressions of fears and wishes are evidence of unconscious opposition. Sometimes we hear of something, only to have the patient leave it unclarified or omitted. Sometimes we know an event or experience was due to occur, but the patient makes no reference to it. Sometimes we can make sense of the associations up to a certain point and then no more. Omissions of the expected are valuable indicators of resistance. At times the only evidence for resistance can be found in the stillness of the analytic experience. The resistance has been sufficient to deprive the associations of affective significance or to drive the thrust of free association into action, outside the analysis. Another group of resistances can be recognized only by their success in preventing any new insight or change to occur. Repetition is the hallmark of this kind of resistance.

Another way of formulating the resistances is in terms of the company they keep. Sometimes they appear as simple, sharply defined obstacles, readily loosened by the analyst's interpretive description. At other times they are evidently a part of a complex network of special interests and fears, like the members of a political party which we oppose. One by one, in the daily campaign of analysis, we seek to separate them from one another, to win them over, and to deprive the organization of its power, even if a few diehards remain. At the extreme, there are those resistances that the patient can overcome only when insight and willpower are ultimately combined, as when a child learning to play chess discovers how king and rook mate the opposing king by forcing him to the board's edge.

In a still different frame of reference, we distinguish the transference resistances from all others because of their special features of involving the analyst. Here it is a case of action within the analysis rather than outside it. Analysis of transference—not only of transference as resistance—is so central that much of the psychoanalytic literature seems to say that what Freud first regarded as an obstacle to treatment is now the goal of all analytic measures. For me, promotion of transference reactions is one of the cardinal consequences of the free association method, not its goal. I take this matter up, again, in chapter 9, where I discuss the criteria for the concept of transference in terms of the free association method. Here it is sufficient to recognize that one group of consequences of the free association method has the feature of re-creating for the patient, in the relationship to the analyst and to the analysis, past experiences with someone else. Such transferences may also operate as unconscious obstacles, regardless of whether they concern positive, affectionate relationships or hostile, negative ones. In these resistances, the patient's unconscious intention to satisfy transference wishes tends to take precedence over his original commitment to the free association method. The analysis of these resistances requires the most demanding rigor of the analyst's neutrality and anonymity to sustain the credibility of his interpretive interventions.

This brings me to a consideration of negative attitudes, conscious hostile and critical thoughts and feelings, toward the analyst and the analysis. Of these, the most interesting are the negative transference reactions. It is important, however, to be aware of other kinds of negative attitudes and to keep in mind that negative attitudes are not necessarily accompanied by reluctance or resistance. On the contrary, sometimes the patient can hardly wait to express his anger, and even when he pauses, believing he has said it all, another sally bursts forth. Or the patient may be reluctant only insofar as he does not wish to express any hostile or critical thought toward the analyst, but the associations betray him, as they should.

Among the sources of negative attitudes are errors, mostly unrecognized, that the analyst has made. That such errors may be, and usually are, given special significance by the patient according to prevailing transference conditions does not vitiate their reality. Occasionally, in a different type of negative attitude, which represents displacement of anger rather than negative transference, the analyst is merely the nearest dog to kick. Frequently the analyst is seen by the patient as the representative of one aspect of the patient himself; for example, the patient may view the analyst as though he stood for one side of an inner conflict. The analyst may then be seen as a dirty old man, tempting the patient into lasciviousness, or as a harsh critic, who wants nothing more for the patient than that he should conform to the standards of an alien society. Such externalizations, "subspecies of transference," as Anna Freud (1965, p. 43) has called them, bring us finally to transference itself as a source of negative attitudes toward analyst and analysis.

Both loving and hostile transferences can lead to negative attitudes in analysis. Such attitudes occur in the direct expression of the hostile transferences, while they result from attempts to ward off loving transferences. For example, a young woman, in the third month of analysis, has revived an intense early childhood love for her father. She complains that she feels her heart beating in the hour. She would like to believe she is frozen, she says, but she knows it isn't so. She begins the next session by saying, "I feel like I want to go or have you leave the room. I don't want to talk. I feel very anxious." In the course of the hour she speaks of a "flood" of thoughts coming to mind, of someone knocked down and injured by the waves at the beach, and then, by way of showers with her boyfriend, she recalls the cherished memory of showers with her father as a little girl. This proves to be the immediate source for the wish that one of us leave the analytic session. I point out that she implies in her associations that the showers were a mixed blessing.

The expression of negative transference is as varied as the modes of free association that convey it. As elsewhere, we aim to expand and to enrich the expression of what is condensed, disguised, or otherwise diminished in intensity. But we are aware that to do so risks development of reluctance to participate in the free association method as we help the patient to reexperience the past. In the easy instances such reluctance remains at the level of verbal criticism or the wish to desert the analysis or to be silent, with clues to meaning in abundance. Those who have experienced its full bitterness, however, will be most likely to appreciate the battlefield image that Freud regularly applied to the analysis of negative transference. Here, more than anywhere else in psychoanalysis, in my experience, the analyst must be certain of his compassionate neutrality in order to be free to take energetic interpretive measures at one point and to be patiently silent at the next.

In this discussion of the varieties of opposition to the free association method, I have omitted consideration of one of their most powerful sources, unconscious guilt, or, as it appears in the free associations, unconscious self-criticism, which I shall take up in the next chapter.

6

The Dynamics of Free Association

The conditions that we choose for analytic work serve to promote the transition from reporting events outside the analysis to experiencing thoughts, feelings, sensations, images, and memories within it. These conditions passively permit rather than actively stimulate free association. They depend for their effect upon a tendency on the patient's part to act, which is channeled in analysis mainly into verbal expression. This tendency to act provides what I called the thrust of the free associations. In this chapter I focus on the interaction of thrust and opposition and on other inner influences that lead to expression or to failure of expression.

It is easiest to grasp those combinations that reflect frustrated wishes and self-imposed restrictions. This is where psychoanalysis began and where the relationship of thrust and opposition are most readily defined. Here, analysis of the free associations refers to the activity of resolving compromise formations into their component parts, brought into consciousness. Condensations are expanded, displacements are brought back to their beginnings, isolated fragments are rejoined, disowned attitudes are reclaimed, reversals are set right, the forgotten is remembered, and so on. This is the analysis of the resistances or, in the structural model of Freud's theory of the mind, the analysis of the defenses and the liberation of repressed wishes and their derivatives.

Much of analytic discourse can be formulated by this paradigm alone, where the tendency for expression and the conditions of the analytic setting are allied. Time is on the side of the bipartisan coalition of patient and analyst, the pace varies according to the patient's needs, and forward motion seldom requires undue strain. Nor is the relationship between thrust and opposition in the free associations fundamentally altered—though the analysis becomes more intense and more difficult—when the patient's tendency to act focuses on the analyst with the imperative force of childhood demands in transference reactions. Even when strongly hostile negative attitudes enter the picture, advantage is on the side of the therapeutic alliance, which gains in strength with the exercise of its influence in the course of analysis.

The free association method runs into difficulty when the imbalance between thrust and opposition is very great, when either one side or the other appears to be absent. In these circumstances it is hard to know how to assist in the expansion of the free associations. They seem either to have achieved an unimpeded condition or to be hopelessly restricted. While the latter provides a positive signal for the analyst that something is awry, the former does not usually do so. It is much harder to recognize the systematic influence of resistances that smoothly and specifically impede a circumscribed area of association while all the rest remains at liberty. Fluency does not guarantee a favorable balance between thrust and resistance. That either case may, in fact, be beyond the capacity of the free association method to alter, whether in the hands of the particular analyst and patient or of any analyst and the patient, at this time or ever, must always be an early consideration. On the other hand, the history of psychoanalytic technique can be seen to develop from the solution of one problem to the next in altering the balance between thrust and opposition, especially in the understanding of forms of opposition that had not previously been recognized.

To understand the dynamics of free association it is necessary to take into account more than a vector analysis of thrust and opposition. Analytic work, especially in the last half century, has brought evidence for a host of influences on free association. These include such qualities and functions as trusting another person, tolerating delay and ambiguity, verbalizing thoughts and thinking abstractly, comprehending multiple meanings, distinguishing fantasy from reality, reflecting upon and integrating experience, and so on. It has, further, demonstrated that those influences have a complicated history in the development of the individual, a history bound up with meaning but also relatively independent of meaning, relatively autonomous. Here is another of the intrinsic uncertainties of the free association method, for just as we have no independent measure of thrust and opposition, we have no way of knowing in advance to what extent or how these essential influences on free association are fixed or modifiable.

I do not propose to review all the findings of ego psychology. Many are incorporated without specific reference throughout these pages. My aim is to emphasize, rather, that the phenomena subsumed under the structural theory of id, ego, and superego must and can be taken into account in the initial understanding of the free associations. (I refer here to the clinical data that Freud's [1923] theory embraces [Hartmann, 1964; Hartmann et al., 1964; E. Kris, 1975; Arlow and Brenner, 1964], not to the particular formulations and metaphors of his structural concepts.) The essential steps in technique connected with this understanding were the extension of the analyst's interest from content of the free associations alone to their context and form, to their interrelated development in the history of the individual, and to the way they reflect the patient's organization of experience.

One important advance in psychoanalytic understanding, the role of unconscious guilt,[1] so significant in the negative therapeutic reactions (Freud, 1923), deserves further consideration because it highlights certain problems in the free association method. These problems result from the insidious nature of unconscious guilt. Like a highly placed traitor, it works its poison from within upon a willing victim, who embraces his supposed ally, redoubles his security measures, and becomes ever more isolated and vulnerable.

It is useful to note some differences between conscious and unconscious guilt, for it is striking to see in retrospect the intensity of the struggle to bring punitive unconscious self-criticisms into conscious awareness (A. Kris, 1976). The operation

---

1. The semantic problems of unconscious "feelings of guilt," "sense of guilt," or, even, "belief in one's guilt" have led me to speak, no more correctly, of unconscious guilt. For me it always signifies punitive unconscious self-criticism.

of unconscious guilt in neurotic individuals tends to be similar to the conscious sense of guilt of psychotic individuals in respect to two matters: the belief that the criticism is wholly justified and the near certainty that others share this view or would if they knew the truth. Unconscious guilt regularly causes some interference with the individual's sense of reality and capacity to make realistic appraisals, in analysis and outside it. Very frequently the analyst's first attempts to demonstrate unconscious self-criticism lead to the belief that the analyst is critical of the patient, to rationalization, to disavowal, and to other attempts to ward off what is experienced by the patient as an attack. From the patient's point of view this attempt on the part of the analyst seems to lead only to intolerable affective experiences, shame, humiliation,[2] rejection, and utter loneliness. The analyst, as usual, attempts to help the patient expand the meanings of these fears, but the task is often formidable, working against powerful forms of reluctance and resistance. Ultimately this expansion must lead to the recognition of why the patient is self-critical now and what have been the reasons for self-criticism throughout his lifetime.

When unconscious guilt is associated with other disorders, in the development of the capacity for personal relationships, especially in regard to becoming independent, or in gratification through punishment (masochism), or in states of depression, the task requires long and arduous periods of repetition and working through in the transference. The analysis of the lonely, young, divorced man who twice dreamed of damage to his car (chap. 3) illustrated the persistence of self-critical attitudes. He criticized himself for masturbation, present and past, and for wanting to be loved, by mother, by other women, and by me. Neither a perversion, as he thought, nor masochistic tendencies played a significant role, but depression and loss were deeply entwined with self-criticism and led, secondarily, to some compromise of independence. I shall return to these

---

2. The painful affects—guilt, shame, humiliation, mortification, and embarrassment—share common features and are not always readily distinguishable from one another (Brenner, 1974). I find it useful, however, to distinguish the self-critical judgments from the frightening anticipations in trying to help patients expand their meanings.

matters in chapter 9, in considering the relationship between externalization and transference, that is, in the clarification of the difference between the present action of unconscious self-criticism and the revival of an old relationship of being criticized or feeling criticized.

Here I want to consider an alternative approach on the part of the analyst to the analysis of unconscious guilt. That is, the analyst might make no intervention and wait until the pressure for expression grows to a point where the patient experiences more relief than anxiety from the demonstration of unconscious self-criticism. Why treat unconscious guilt differently from other unconscious obstacles to free association? Time, after all, is on the side of the therapeutic alliance in those instances. So far as it is successful, this approach is, in fact, the one that is first adopted by the analyst in dealing with unconscious guilt, too.

The problem of unconscious guilt hinges on the patient's assumption that the analyst must share his critical opinion. Generally, the more the patient may wish to express whatever triggers unconscious guilt, the more this assumption perpetuates opposition to free association. Thrust and opposition are then closely balanced, but expression tends to diminish the therapeutic alliance when the patient assumes that the analyst will withdraw from the coalition in the process. Silence on the part of the analyst is taken for agreement in these matters and will serve only to stifle the free associations.

The question for the analyst is how to promote free association in the direction of clarifying unconscious guilt without yielding to the temptation, as Freud put it, "to play the part of prophet, saviour, and redeemer to the patient" (1923, p. 50, n.). I am aware that in this instance I seem to be contradicting my earlier injunction against the analyst as interpreter assuming that he has some insight that he must wait to give the patient at some right moment. The situation, as I see it, is not that the analyst knows it all from the start. Far from it. He is in fact most often surprised to discover that the patient makes the assumption that he is critical, or, worse, finds that he has unwittingly agreed with the patient's self-criticism.

In the analysis of one severely needy, depressed, self-critical man, who summarized his situation in an unintended pun on his first name, "I can't fill the bill," I learned a valuable lesson. I had thought that after a very lengthy period of treatment I understood the extent of his self-criticism and the way he punished himself for his inadequacies. He complained one day that he was not giving enough time or interest to his son. I drew the connection between this observation of his and the ones that he regularly omitted, how little he had been given as a child and how little he was getting now. Several weeks later, when we were both keenly aware that the free associations had come to a grinding halt, he agreed with my guess that he had taken my comment only as a confirmation of his own belief of his inadequacy as a father. In retrospect it seems that I had missed the point—admittedly, well concealed—that he was presenting his self-evaluation in order to be criticized by me. Whether there was any way to convey such an insight without his first painfully enacting it in the relationship to me, I am not sure.

Successful and unsuccessful attempts have led me to conclude that the analysis of unconscious guilt depends, ultimately, upon the transference revival of childhood love for those who were the models for the development of standards. This revival, however, depends in part on the analyst's ability to help the patient distinguish his actual views from those critical ones that the patient attributes to him. Positive attitudes are rarely sufficient from the first for such patients to recognize that the analyst is not critical.

If silence is confirmation, contradiction alone is no better, for it tends only to close the door to further association. The analyst must actively demonstrate the operation of unconscious guilt, as he learns to recognize it in the patient's self-punitive actions and, especially, in the apathetic reluctance and provocative negativism that are frequently its only signs. In doing so the analyst needs to be explicit in pointing out that he is not critical of the patient. On such occasions, when clarification is needed to help the patient sort out the realistic from the unrealistic, the gains outweigh the potential loss to the analysis of transference. So long as the analyst's point of view is expressed solely in the service of the patient's needs and not out of an intolerance of negative transference, for example, it conforms to my understanding of the need for anonymity on the part of the analyst.

This consideration has brought us close to the problem of gratification and the rule of abstinence in analytic work, which I shall take up in the next chapter. It has also reminded us that analytic work is very nearly circular in requiring the analysis of unconscious guilt for the development of positive transference and positive transference for the analysis of unconscious guilt. The solution depends on taking small steps over a long period of time. The rate of progress, in any case, is hour by hour.

7

Satisfaction in Free Association

Psychoanalysis, from the very beginning, addressed itself to the problem of the patient's experience. It began with the question of what is excluded from the patient's experience and what sustains the exclusion. The first hypothesis, that trauma occurring in one kind of consciousness, the hypnoid state, cannot be recalled in ordinary consciousness, soon gave way to a theory of repression and unconscious conflict, with an ego concept that Freud, like Griesinger (1845) before him, borrowed from Johann F. Herbart. The extraordinary findings about mental life that were made with the theory of repression in this form in the first 30 years of Freud's psychoanalytic work prepared the way for the psychoanalytic study of character. The revision of Freud's earlier theories in the structural theory (1923) focused attention on the functions and organization of the ego and paved the way for a psychoanalytic view of mental life and development not wholly linked to conflict. A further essential function of the revised theory was to acknowledge the requirement for a study of experience and its development, especially the experience of affects. In this chapter I approach the problem of the experience of free association from that perspective.

One of the questions that psychoanalysts have put to themselves over and over is why patients are willing to go through the arduous procedure of psychoanalysis. There have been many partial answers. To begin with there is the conscious motivation for relief of symptoms or the need for change. There is the friendly interest of the analyst, with pleasure in the prospect of joint venture, which continues in the therapeutic alliance. There is the appeal of concentrated attention when only the patient is to be the focus of interest, and there is the group of positive transferences to give it intensity. Hope, which is certainly an essential therapeutic ingredient, derives from all of these. The enormous satisfaction of feeling understood, the excitement of growing insight, and greater understanding of oneself contribute significantly to the forces that sustain the patient's motivation. In this chapter I want to emphasize the additional experience of satisfaction in the *activity* of free association.

For example, early in his analysis a warm but most obsessional young man, who works an extremely long day as is customary for ambitious members of his profession, begins a session by saying that he wasted yesterday's hour. Then he complains that when he gets home and wants to take a nap, his wife cajoles him into doing chores and paying attention to her. She says that he is no fun anymore—always tired. The mornings he comes to his analysis he gets more than an hour's extra sleep. As the youngest child in his family, he says, he developed faster than his brothers and sisters. I suggest that he wishes to be alone and quiet, that he likes the opportunity in analysis to be free from the pressure of intruders and the demand to march, march, march. He recalls the pleasures of living alone in a garret when he was in college. He has lost that and will never regain it. He says that he often uses my observations to prod himself; for instance, my observation that comfort in analysis is a time of resistance. I remind him that the comment he refers to (in an earlier session) had quoted *his* point of view. My own view, I add, again, is that the more comfortable he is, the more likely he is to think about what he wants. He then quotes the friend who had originally suggested he consider analytic treatment: "When you're comfortable, you're not getting anything out of treatment." I point out his attraction to pressure and to conflict. In college, he says, when he didn't have something to do, he felt uncomfortable; he felt he was missing something. At this point in the hour he finds himself feeling very tense. After a moment's silence he says he has a memory of an experience from when he was thirteen years old. He had entered a new and more difficult school and was assigned an essay on "To Be Great Is to Be Misunderstood." He couldn't think what to write. He paced his room. His father woke up and came in. The patient ended up able to write his paper. His mother came up with useful suggestions. He recalls the intensity of his anxiety. He had assumed that he could just sit down and write, but he couldn't. Ever since he has been compulsive in outlining things. He tries to avoid writing reports and other papers required for work all in one night. That experience at thirteen was important; to be uncomfortable is to get something done. He notes that he was tense in this session, and then the memory came—a case in point. But he says that he was not so good at exams under pressure. I add that memory brought back his parents as helpful. He wants to be sarcastic in reply, he says. They had put him in the private school when he wanted to go to public school.

On the next day, the patient begins by reviewing the sequence of the previous session. He says he was relaxed by the time he drove away. It was reassuring and remarkable. An explicit clarification develops during this second session. The demands made by his wife and the demands of his analyst and the analysis (the new school) are currently equated with the traumatic seductive sexual demands of an older sister in his childhood. His parents had not protected him from her. He had spoken of analysis as respite but, a moment later, contentiously attributed to me his own fear and disapproval of relaxation. To relax was to become susceptible to dangerous excitement, yet he longed to relax. He also wanted to regain the freedom to enjoy excitement. What was reassuring and remarkable in his view, it turned out, was that in the analysis relaxation could lead to tension and to relief, to anxiety and to assistance.

I choose this example because it demonstrates to me the experience of satisfaction in the activity of free association along with satisfaction in the contents, which were mainly concerned with clarification of the difference between childhood trauma and adult analysis. The transference in the first of these sessions was ambivalent, with significant though not unusual reluctance, yet the signs of free association were clearly present. The experience of tension within the session came without any conscious direction, as did the memory that followed. The associations were intelligible, and the organizing principle or principles could be formulated—better after the next session, but well enough at the time. Finally, there was the experience of satisfaction in the activity of free association, which occurs most clearly when a resistance has been analyzed and thereby overcome.

This example gives me another opportunity to consider the question of alternative formulations and alternative styles of intervention. When the patient attributed to me the injunction against comfort in the analysis, I took it as an externalization of his own view—which I had, in fact, pointed out to him before. When I had said it earlier, I did not foresee the double transference context of ambivalence about excitement in seduction and about his parents who pressured him to grow up too fast, who failed to protect him but also helped elsewhere. Nor did I recognize the negative parental transference until the second session, which I summarized briefly. Would it then have been better to allow his error to stand, to let the negative transference grow, or, if one was to intervene, to interpret the misattribution as a parental transference? One could have pointed out that he first spoke of growing up fast as the youngest child, but that he then felt pressured to give up comfort. In another direction, his memory of the paper he was to write, "To Be Great Is to Be Misunderstood," may have referred to his own error about what I had said earlier regarding comfort in analysis. Perhaps he was feeling grateful to his analyst, whom he had misunderstood. Then, after a tense moment, he may have been paying his analyst a compliment that way, which was further elaborated the next day in the feeling of a remarkable experience. Some might regard this development, in the direction of idealization, as the most important part of this analytic experience.

My own approach, as I indicated in the last chapter, is influenced by a high index of suspicion for the presence of unconscious self-criticism, its externalization, and a belief that the analyst will hold a similar critical view. I think it was important to clarify the confusion based on his externalization. I can offer in support—though hardly proof—that the patient responded with expansion of the associations and of the transference. The focus of his attention, early in analysis, was on whether analysis would be safe or dangerous; to allow a confusion of such proportions to remain, in the service of possible advantages in transference potential, risks far more than it stands to gain, in my opinion. Confusion of this sort is one of the characteristic disorders of the sense of reality that result from the action of unconscious guilt in neurosis. Some analysts might have thought it sufficient to clarify the intent of my comment from the earlier session, to show him that I had been pointing out his view, without any statement about my own. They might feel that stating my opinion on the importance of comfort in analysis verges too close upon suggestion, and that it might therefore restrict free association to some extent. There is room for difference of opinion.

In this patient, as in others, there were several sources of unconscious guilt. Where such guilt is particularly linked with conflicts over separation and bodily autonomy, which was not a major factor for him, the self-criticism is sometimes so great as to interfere with the ordinary capacity for recognizing dissatisfaction in daily life. Such patients often ask whether their associations are really free associations, for they cannot tell by the affective signal that others take for granted. It is as though they do not have a right to know their own feelings. It is from these patients that I have learned most about the extraordinary experience of satisfaction in free association, as they gradually regain their rights. From them, too, I have learned to notice dissatisfaction as a sign of interference with free association. Naturally, it is always difficult to distinguish dissatisfaction in the activity of free association from dissatisfaction in the transference or in other contents of the associations, but it is, nonetheless, a valuable distinction.

In the example cited, the patient began the session by criticizing himself for wasting the previous analytic hour. In one way, he was being characteristically hard on himself. He had little patience with loafing on the job, and analysis was work, no doubt of it, for him. But he was also speaking out of dissatisfaction, since free association had not yet brought the satisfaction he was about to achieve.

The importance which I attach to the experience of satisfaction in sustaining the patient's motivation in analysis brings up the problem of other forms of satisfaction. For example, it is hard for me to conceive of the expression of fantasy and wish or the experience of strong feelings, positive or negative, about the analyst, which is not to some extent satisfying—though each may also become frightening, disappointing, and frustrating. The activity of free association can be satisfying, even when the substance of the communication is most unhappy. In my opinion, the more satisfying the patient finds the experience of free association, the more likely he is to follow his associations wherever they lead, to look to the associations for the answers to his questions in analysis, and to tolerate the inevitable frustrations imposed by the method of free association.

Is there a place for abstinence in psychoanalysis? I think there is. While satisfaction in free association can operate as a powerful source of motivation in analysis, it can also become a vehicle of resistance. It is, in fact, characteristic of transference wishes that patients will try to pursue their satisfaction to the exclusion of the analytic goals. The analyst has the task at such points of reminding the patient of his original commitment to free association and to assist the patient in expanding his awareness of the transference wishes. The rule of abstinence, it seems to me, is no more than a summary of the analyst's functions in the free association method, while he remains neutral with respect to the patient's conflicts and relinquishes other proprietary rights. To gratify the patient's wishes or to fail to assist the patient in expanding the free associations would be to abandon the responsibilities of the analyst.

Finally, there are certain matters of analytic style and of personality among analysts which are particularly likely to appear as differences in regard to satisfaction in analysis. My own style involves a certain freedom to use humor, and I have not found that this has impeded analysis. On occasion, however, I have found patients who would make humor or laughter a vehicle of resistance, and, once, my pleasure in the analysis of dreams led to a patient's repeating with me the seductive exhibitionism of his mother, by providing me with well-orchestrated, though not consciously prepared, dreams and associations for exhibition of my interpretive talents. As in all other instances, when the free associations stagnate, it is time for the analyst to help the patient return to his original analytic aims.

8

Free Association in Two Kinds of Conflict

In reviewing the regulatory influences that impinge upon the free associations, I find it useful to identify two kinds of conflict which may be encountered with the free association method. The formulation of reluctance and resistance in conflict with the thrust of the associations constituted one of Freud's first contributions. It developed into the paradigm of the *conflicts of defense* (1894), in which unwelcome thoughts and feelings are actively kept from consciousness. This model gradually led to the present-day analysis of the defenses, operating as resistances, in which the organization of the defenses, the influences that set and keep them in motion, their history and personal importance in the patient's development, and related considerations are regarded with as great an interest as is accorded the thoughts, wishes, feelings, images, sensations, and memories that have been excluded from awareness. Even the late recognition of unconscious guilt was formulated in terms of such a model.

The analysis of resistance in the conflicts of defense depends upon the persistence of the thrust of free association. Unfulfilled wishes can be counted upon to be expressed through the associations. By their voltage they illuminate the associations like bulbs on a Christmas tree, where telltale darkness identifies points of high resistance. This model, much modified by the study of ego psychology and by the increasing influence of developmental considerations, remains at the center of psychoanalytic technique. I use it here as a model of the regulation of free association, not as a model of the mind (Gedo and Goldberg, 1973), though Freud developed his models of the mind to articulate very closely with this first, experience-near formulation.

The analyst's interventions serve to sharpen the conflict of defense, to concentrate its focus. Sometimes, but not always, this leads to a representation of the conflict in which the wish is addressed to the analyst or the analyst is seen as the agent of defense. Favoring neither wish nor defense, the analyst aims to help the patient express consciously both sides of the conflict. In this process, the patient's feeling of tension regularly mounts until some form of insight is reached and there is a concomitant temporary reduction of tension. More than merely reducing tension, such events are characteristically satisfying and serve to promote the patient's motivation to follow the free associations. New expressions of frustrated wishes can be expected to sustain their thrust.

The second broad group of conflicts encountered with the free association method, the conflicts of ambivalence, were first characterized not as a model of the regulation of free association but in terms of the psychoanalytic theory of instinctual drives. Freud used the term ambivalence mainly to refer to simultaneous feelings of love and hate, though at times he used it to refer to a conflict between active and passive libidinal aims (1915, p. 131, n. 2). Later, with the structural revision of psychoanalytic theory (Freud, 1923), the concept of intrasystemic conflicts covered a still wider range (Rangell, 1963a, 1963b). My own use of the term *conflicts of ambivalence*, as a paradigm of free association, parallels the latter.

For purposes of exposition I shall begin by outlining the scope of Freud's formulations of the conflicts of ambivalence. I have in mind, first, the conflicts between various forms of loving and being loved which may seem to the patient incompatible with one another. Of these conflicts, the ones I have found to be most prevalent are those between wishes to be loved, as small children are loved by their parents, and wishes to love actively, with a focus on genital sexuality. I find it useful to formulate these conflicts in terms of Freud's theory of sexuality (1905), according to the bodily sources, the active and passive aims, the personal objects, and the egoistic, sadistic, and altruistic organizations of the sexual drives. In adolescence, stark conflicts of ambivalence, such as the problems of shifting attachments from one's parents to new figures outside the family and the problems of responding to homosexual and heterosexual interests, require special attention. Those patients who were unable to resolve such conflicts at that developmentally appropriate time need to do so in their analytic development. I shall return briefly to the topic of ambivalence in adolescence in chapter 11, when I take up some additional considerations of free association and development.

The structural revision of Freud's theory of the mind summarized additional groups of conflicts of ambivalence, not immediately connected with instinctual drives, the intrasystemic conflicts within ego and superego. These include, for example, instances in which a wish for excitement and involvement in human relationships raises fears of being overwhelmed by excitement or involvement. A similar kind of intrasystemic conflict in the ego may lead an individual partially or completely to relinquish his realistic appraisals of the external world when such appraisals conflict with a wish to seek gratification at any cost. The executive functions of the ego are often in potential conflict with one another. Similarly, self-protective and self-punitive functions of the superego are often in significant intrasystemic conflict. Here I wish to focus on the scope of conflicts of ambivalence, not their formulation in a theory of the mind. My aim is to consider these conflicts from the viewpoint of free association, that is, to describe conflicts of ambivalence as a paradigm of the regulation of free association.

Conflicts of ambivalence may be manifested in a number of ways in the associations. Two opposing trends may be closely woven together in a compromise formation. For example, an androgynous figure appears in a dream. More commonly, ambivalent wishes are closely linked in a fantasy. In one instance a woman imagines herself sexually assaulted in the waiting room. The fantasy is of a pleasurable, exciting sexual encounter without any responsibility on her part. Unspoken, but part of the background, is a news story from the day before, of a young woman raped in a train station. The crucial missing element in the manifest fantasy is that the woman's parents came from far away to take care of her after the event. Wishes to be taken care of were replaced by masochistic wishes and were secretly enjoyed along with fantasies of guiltless genital sexuality. This fantasy was relatively successful from the point of view of evading unconscious self-criticism in regard to both sides of the ambivalence.

In another form, two sides of an ambivalent conflict may be temporally linked in the associations, sometimes as doing and undoing, sometimes as sequential alternations of wish, mood, or transference. In reactions of hurrying away, for example, a wish to be cared for regularly threatens to be too directly expressed, and a wish to be active and mature carries the patient off at a gallop (A. Kris, 1977). Neither wish is satisfied. If such reactions are formulated as conflicts of defense, the active wishes might be incorrectly viewed as a defense against the passive ones (to be cared for). The problem is better understood in terms of the hallmark of the conflicts of ambivalence, the fear that one side will be expressed without the other. The typical picture in these conflicts is the mutual frustration of the two sides of the conflict.

One group of conflicts of ambivalence is accompanied by a persistent childhood attitude of "either-or." These conflicts, which I have described as either-or dilemmas (1977), appear to the patient to be insoluble because of the threat of loss, no matter what solution he attempts. From these dilemmas, which are regularly composites of several conflicts of ambivalence, it can be most readily seen that the characteristic influence of such conflicts on free association is a reluctance to proceed, out of a fear of loss. The expected loss derives from the *activity* of free association, not from the content or meanings it reveals. The reluctance to proceed often leads to unconscious self-criticism. I find it helpful to alert patients to this self-criticism and to remind them of their fear of loss and of the companion belief that the analyst will agree with their either-or conclusion. Expansion of these thoughts in the associations leads in several directions.

One important direction is the emphasis on "should" and "ought." Self-critical attitudes of diverse origins link up with the injunction to renounce one side of the ambivalence. Among these are the instances in which individuals experience a conflict between their autonomy in regard to bodily wishes and their need for someone's love or protection. A closely related line leads to issues of surrender of self-control. The idea of re-

linquishing conscious control over thought processes, further
augmented by the idea of yielding some of one's self-control to
someone else, poses a significant threat of loss. Another line of
association leads to problems in the development of tolerance
for uncertainty.

The following excerpt illustrates the problem for a patient
caught in multiple either-or dilemmas. A man in his twenties,
unsuccessful, lonely, and feeling defeated, enters analysis after
a period of psychotherapy. In the third month, he begins an
hour, saying, "I feel terrible, physically." Fears and memories
of mistreatment abound, mostly in complaints about his parents. He notices toward the end of the hour that "time is hang-
ing heavy this session." I remind him that a long weekend lies
ahead. He has forgotten. He begins the next session four days
later enthusiastically. He feels torn: he wants to be less defen-
sive, but he feels naked and vulnerable. He thinks of going into
isolation and depriving himself of sleep. If he comes to analysis
in a state of panic, it will be better. His thoughts turn to several
dangers, then to a dream:

> My mother is taking injections for anxiety. I said, "You
> have to face anxiety, not stifle it."

He wanted to feel superior to her. He tells a dream from the
night after the last session:

> I felt like a little boy, though my present age. Mother said I
> could be her boyfriend but later she turned away. I
> pleaded, "You said I could be your boyfriend."

He loves his mother, but he is angry at what he has had to
do to keep her love. He goes on to say he feels very vulnerable in
relation to me and open to criticism. He agrees with my view
that he feels he is back in the situation of a little boy. He extends
this theme, and we clarify the feeling that he sees me as a parent. The longing for me clearly parallels unsatisfied longing to
be cared for by his parents. He volunteers the observation that
he wants to please me. Partly, however, the free associations
are for himself, he says. We also agree that he wants to control
the free associations to avoid painful reexperiences. He adds
that he pretends to be interested in what I say, just as he used to
do with his father. In fact, he feels torn between placating me
and disagreeing. He feels I have problems when he challenges

my authority. Again, he fears criticism, which he feels he deserves. He invites my criticism, I suggest, as a reaction to his feelings of longing over the weekend.

While any number of conflicts of defense are adumbrated, here they are far from analytic accessibility. In this early phase of analysis for this very disturbed young man the conflicts of ambivalence take center stage along with savage self-criticism. One can hardly hope in crosswinds such as these to sail a steady course. It is success enough to keep the process afloat. Gradually the rapid alternations tend to slow down, when some degree of satisfaction is obtained in free association. The wish to be cared for by me gains some slight satisfaction in these two sessions. His attempts to be active in the analysis are much less successful. He wants to impose extra measures, such as sleep deprivation, to be active in free association in response to my absence. He chooses a characteristically self-punitive approach.

Three measures serve most significantly to assist the patient in resolving the conflicts of ambivalence. The first is to help the patient recognize the degree of frustration that remains, despite partial solutions. This applies equally to events outside the analysis and within it. For example, the man who divides his loving between one woman whose body he adores and another who shares his love of books and ideas needs to recognize his dissatisfaction with this arrangement in order to understand its several meanings. The banker who denigrates me and psychoanalysis but dreams that Austrian bonds are going to lose interest needs to know that he wants more from me than he dares to let himself think of. Satisfaction is greatest when both sides of the ambivalence can be kept in mind at the same time and brought to resolution.

The second therapeutic measure, and by far the most important, is the expression through free association of both sides of the ambivalence. The natural inclination of the patient will be to withdraw from free association, when expression of one side alone leads to increasing tension. The analyst must therefore assist the patient in expressing both sides alternately. I picture the activity of free association following the swings of a gradually lengthening pendulum that spends longer and longer periods of time on each side. Where things go well, a person who begins analysis enmeshed in ambivalence, unable to express either friendly or unfriendly thoughts alone, may gradually be able to tolerate a sustained attempt to express either one. As the wishes on each side are expressed, they become subject to conflicts of defense. Ironically, when a patient who has been unable to resolve conflicts between homosexual and heterosexual wishes has freed up his active wishes for genital sexuality with a woman, his reward in analysis is to become subject to revived fears of his father in the transference. Similarly, such patients may at first be unable to develop a father transference alone or mother transference alone or transference from a single period of development. Gradually, they may come to tolerate relatively isolated extended transference reactions. I shall return to this observation in the next two chapters. Here I want to emphasize the role of satisfaction in free association, first on one side and then on the other in successive alternation, as a specific therapeutic measure for conflicts of ambivalence. It reverses the mutual frustration of the ambivalent wishes and attitudes.

The third therapeutic measure follows with little effort in most instances from the second. Once the components of ambivalence have been released from each other's crippling embrace, they need to be brought together once again in conscious resolution, on terms not dictated by conditions of frustration. Such resolution, compromise, and synthesis can usually be made with little pain or sense of loss, even though something has to be given up. It is a curious paradox that once wishes have been satisfied, they can be relinquished. They do not lead to the rampant addiction that the patient fears will deprive him of one side or the other. Where the prerequisites for resolution of ambivalence, tolerance of tension, delay, and uncertainty are insufficient, the patient may need assistance to develop them in order to complete resolution of the conflicts of ambivalence.

I want to close this chapter with a comparison of the two paradigms of conflict in free association. The hallmark of the conflicts of ambivalence is the anticipation of loss through the activity of free association. The analysis of conflicts of defense may also lead to anticipation of loss, but in their case it is because of the contents and meanings of the associations. For example, expression of a wish to emulate the analyst is frequently followed by fear of loss through rejection or punitive retaliation by the analyst. In the conflicts of ambivalence it is the activity of free association rather than its content that leads to the fear of loss. Although patients sometimes rationalize these fears, clarification demonstrates that what they fear is always the loss of the other side of the ambivalence. If the analyst approaches one side of a conflict of ambivalence as though it were a conflict of defense alone, the result is increasing reluctance. If this approach proceeds, unnoticed, the patient is apt to take the analyst's interventions as endorsement of self-criticism directed toward the other side of the ambivalence.

Historically, psychoanalysis began as the attempt to help the patient *remember* in the conflicts of defense, through the analysis of resistance and transference. As interest focused on the study of obsessional neurosis and melancholia (e.g., Freud, 1909, 1913, 1917), three concepts were brought together: ambivalence, loss, and interrupted mourning. I find it useful to formulate their relationship from the viewpoint of free association as it operates in conflicts of ambivalence. In these conflicts, free association regularly encounters the sense of loss as either side alone attempts to gain expression and satisfaction without the other. From this perspective, conflicts of ambivalence are states of loss dynamically sustained by mutual frustration of paired wishes and attitudes. Resolution of ambivalence through free association requires more than remembering. It requires tolerance of the sense of loss as each side gains expression. By making conscious what was previously unconscious and by focusing attention on what had earlier been avoided, free association leads at first only to painful awareness and reluctance to go forward. Free association must therefore proceed in very small steps, first on one side and then on the other of the conflicts of ambivalence. In doing so, however, it follows the form of mourning outside analysis. In those situations, the painful recall of myriad small memories leads one to regain a portion of oneself that has been lost on account of its intimate connection with the object of one's affection. From the viewpoint of free association, *mourning* is the aspect of memory required in the resolution of conflicts of ambivalence, where remembering is the aspect required in conflicts of defense.

Viewed from another perspective, mourning can be defined as the painful surrender of the illusion of permanence, principally the permanence of those one loves and of oneself. This illusion favors one portion of an individual's experience over another, preserving a sense of continuity in relationships at the expense of the sense of reality. Mourning is in that way the activity which leads to the resolution of a conflict of ambivalence between the intolerance of loss and the inner requirements for the integrity of experience.

One additional complication and interaction cannot be avoided in discussing the relationship of these two kinds of conflicts. When memory of traumatic experiences and the origins of conflicts of defense have been recovered through free association, the revision of old solutions does not always yield so easily as one might hope. The old solutions regularly include pathways of gratification for childhood wishes that do not conform to the patient's present standards. Two forms or organizations of loving or two aspects of self-image may now be in conflict—a conflict of ambivalence. That is, the successful analysis of conflicts of defense often requires analysis of conflicts of ambivalence in the process of working through, in the same way that resolution of conflicts of ambivalence may permit analysis of the conflicts of defense in the separated components.

9

Transference and Free Association

Just as psychoanalysis does not create free association in the treatment setting, it does not create the tendency to develop transference reactions. It does, however, systematically alter the balance of influences on free association in favor of the expression of memory in this form. The concept of transference holds a central position in psychoanalysis. My aim, here, is to present the rationale for a formulation of transference from the viewpoint of free association and to demonstrate the clinical distinctions it facilitates.

Transference, like resistance, is inferred and therefore requires definition of its limits. Psychoanalysts, starting with Freud, have employed various, overlapping definitions, explicitly and implicitly. The definition which I present here derives from clinical psychoanalysis, and it is linked closely to genetic interpretation. That is, an interpretation relating to revival of past experience rather than one relating only to present conditions is the characteristic intervention when transference dominates the free associations. In formulating the definition I have abstracted from the determinants of free association in situations where genetic interpretation has proved relevant.

My definition of transference circumscribes a form of free association whose organizing principle has three basic elements: (1) the direct operation of an unconscious memory of a relationship; (2) the unconscious re-creation of this old relationship so that thoughts, feelings, wishes, sensations, and images are directed toward the analyst and the analysis in place of the person or, less frequently, the nonhuman partner (e.g., an animal or an institution) involved in the original relationship; and (3) a tendency to disrupt the agreement for analysis, to reject the constraints of verbal free association, to affirm the misperceptions of the analyst as reality, to redress old injuries, and to seek gratification rather than reexperience old frustrations.

This definition, as will be evident, emphasizes the direct influence of unconscious memory on the associations rather than an unconscious focus on the analyst. In limiting transference to those instances in which a memory of a relationship operates as the immediate organizing principle of the associations, it sacrifices the valuable use of the term to embrace all reactions in which the associations reveal a distortion of the patient's view of the relationship between the patient and the analyst. By including the tendency to disrupt the agreement for analysis, it excludes those elements of rapport between patient and analyst that many analysts (e.g., Stone, 1961; Zetzel, 1971, chap. 12; Greenson, 1967) regard as an essential positive transference from early childhood. It disregards, too, those of Freud's formulations that view transference as the basis of all relationships and the decisive factor in the influence of the physician (e.g., 1925, p. 42) and follows Freud's earlier, narrower formulations of transference (e.g., 1905, pp. 116–17) more closely. I find myself in agreement with others, such as Hendrick (1958, p. 194) and Anna Freud (1968), from whose position mine derives. This position shares the view generally held that early good relationships are necessary for the development of rapport between patient and analyst and for relationships in general. It rejects the assumption, however, that childhood memory operates *directly* and unconsciously in these instances, rather than through the intervention of organized aspects of the adult personality. In any event, I cannot see that the method of free association could provide direct evidence in regard to this difference of opinion, since such relatively unambivalent feelings as the trusting matrix of analytic rapport do not enter the free associations in a way that reveals their immediate origin. I prefer, therefore, to leave open the question of how memory and the organized aspects of the adult personality, identifications and enduring character traits, may interact in producing rapport.

The essential question to which the first part of my definition of transference addresses itself may be stated as follows: is the organizing principle of the patient's associations an unconscious memory of a past relationship, operating directly, or is it an organized part of the adult personality, operating in a similar, unconscious fashion? Only where an unconscious memory is the direct basis of the organizing principle will the analyst's efforts to link present behavior with past experience facilitate expansion of the free associations. This definition of transference immediately distinguishes transference from three groups of similar reactions that focus on the analyst: (1) those influenced by present-day hopes, wishes, fears, and other expectations; (2) those that represent characteristic patterns of behavior; and (3) those that derive from externalization of one aspect of inner conflict. (Comparable distinctions are made by Sandler et al., 1975, 1980.) In all of these situations, interpretation of the associations as evidence of childhood experience can only dissuade the patient from attaching any importance to understanding unconscious aspects of his present feelings. At worst it can mask self-criticism, induce compliance, and prevent resolution of conflicts of ambivalence.

A man to whom analysis was unfamiliar, who knew nobody who had been analyzed, began his first hour commenting on the awkwardness and discomfort he felt at lying before me on the couch. He wondered whether he would lose control over his life and how submissive he would have to be. His thoughts turned to one of his enduring interests, which involved activities that his father regarded as unimportant. He went on to complain that his father was extremely domineering and cited a number of examples.

I believe that most analysts would recognize in such an hour the patient's anxious concern over whether his analyst was going to be as disapproving and domineering as his father. That question does not, I believe, derive from unconscious memory operating directly. It is principally the adult patient consciously and unconsciously formulating his question about present experience in terms of past experience. I do not regard this as transference, because the memory of the past experience is not unconscious and the past experience is recalled rather than revived in the present relationship to the analyst. Furthermore, the tendency to disrupt the agreement for analysis, which I regard as characteristic of transference, is absent. There is, however, the first evidence of a marked neurotic pattern of surrendering control and fighting to regain it. In my view, only the fear of domination could usefully be expanded by drawing his attention to his concerns of being controlled by me as he felt controlled by his father.

I shall not repeat here my previous remarks on externalization. In the case of unconscious self-criticisms I believe it is especially important to recognize the distinction between transference, the present revival of a past experience of feeling criticized, and externalization, attributing to the analyst a current self-critical attitude. In my experience these two forms of association may appear more or less simultaneously in the course of analysis, although the one that appears more accessible to me, earlier, is usually the externalized self-criticism. Where we are concerned with the recall of childhood experience, as it leads to the development of unreasonably severe self-critical attitudes, I find that we need to rely on the patient's familiarity with self-criticism in analyzing the transference reactions of feeling criticized.

A woman whose expression of aggressive intention was severely limited in all areas came a few minutes late to a number of sessions, although for several years she had always arrived promptly without fail. I wondered whether it was part of a nascent hostile transference, a first attempt, with few verbal cues. Hoping to promote further associations, I drew her attention to the tardiness. Although there was no suggestion of criticism in what I said, nor any covert criticism, she took umbrage at my comment and vigorously (for her) defended her record of punctuality. I was able to help her see that the criticism she attributed to me was her own, pointing out that it was precisely the change from punctuality that led me to wonder if the tardiness held meaning. The expression of a hostile transference was still some time off.

When the negative transference appeared, it too was initiated by an attribution, but this time, in due course, it was followed by revival of past experience. A number of suggestive dreams led this woman, now well versed in analytic ways, to begin a particular hour with the accusation that I would say that she suffered from penis envy. It happened that the analysis had quite successfully revived the events of the early oedipal years, and although a tonsillectomy, a woman's broken nose, and a miscarriage had been linked with masturbation and cas-tration themes, no evidence for significant penis envy had been forthcoming. This may have been due to a specially good rela-tionship with her mother during that phase of her develop-ment. After the statement of accusation we both laughed at her caricature of analysis, for she knew well enough from previous considerations that I was not likely to jump to such a conclu-sion. On the other hand, we both had to admit that it did sound like penis envy in the dreams. We stayed our interpretive zeal until the associations brought, in another dream, the evidence we were looking for: memories of her envy of a brother, born when she was nearly seven years old. She now remembered a forgotten year of her life in which she felt she lost both her parents, father to illness, mother to the baby. By that age, not only was the time for penis envy behind her, the severity of established, autonomous self-critical functions would not per-mit the expression of resentment. Whole chunks of experience disappeared from conscious memory along with her freedom to assert herself and to use her intellectual faculties fully until they gradually returned during analysis. Anger poured out, mostly in the mother transference. Naturally, she also ex-pressed criticisms of her anger and of her infantile wishes. As she attributed these criticisms to me, we found that they re-flected her childhood experience more than they expressed any current self-criticism. She developed, in fact, a new sym-pathy with herself by applying her current tolerance to the emerging picture of herself as a child and became a better mother to herself.

When I speak of the revival or re-creation of childhood ex-perience in the transference, there is no implication that the relationship was "objectively" as critical as the patient felt it to be. Transference reproduces experience as it is remembered. The question of who did what to whom, which is always a most important part of the reconstruction of the past, and often a most difficult one, requires additional data.

Much of the second element of my definition of transfer-ence has already been touched upon in these examples. I have not yet discussed the form of reproduction of past relationships in transference reactions, however, and it seems important to do so. It is rare in my experience to see transference reactions right at the beginning of analysis—though, again, I stress that there are other kinds of reaction focused on the analyst. As the first transference reactions develop, they tend to show several characteristics that distinguish them from later ones. They tend to be briefer and less intense, and they tend to condense or to synthesize memories of several relationships or several phases in the relationship with one person. That is one area in which the free association method analyzes, in the narrow sense of the word, separating the elements of complex reactions and gradually allowing each the opportunity for full expression in free association.

I described earlier (chap. 5) an episode from the third month of the analysis of a young woman, in which the excitement of showers she had taken in childhood with her father was revived in the analytic session. The "flood" of thoughts was a double reference, to water in the showers and to the dangerously mounting excitement. There was an unconscious memory of the past relationship, although the showers themselves and her pleasure in them had not been forgotten. The unconscious memory was of the anxiety she had experienced and of her own wish to leave the showers. She had regretted the termination of that close relationship with her father, and much of the subsequent analytic course was concerned with her resentment and low self-esteem. For this woman penis envy played a major role. When much of this territory had been covered, more than three years later, and she and her boyfriend were at last, in the fashion of the times, contemplating marriage because they wanted to have a child together, the theme of the showers returned in the transference.

The patient arrives at a winter hour complaining of heat and exhaustion. After a few minutes she says again, "I'm so hot ... I have to get out of here." She asks if it is hot in the room, and I tell her the thermometer reads seventy-two degrees. She continues: to her it feels like an inferno; she needs to breathe cold air; now she feels cold; she can't talk today; she has to get a drink of water. At this point she leaves the office and gets a drink of water in the bathroom. When she is back on the couch, she supposes that she must be anxious. She refers to making love without her diaphragm but turns to her fear that I must be irritated. A moment later she says she is shivering. Then she thinks of her period: it smells funny. Her boyfriend's penis is irritating in her vagina, which is dry. I interpolate, "Oh," and she replies, "The drink of water!" She equates dryness in sex and in talking and continues with further review of sexual problems in her associations. Toward the end of the hour she notes that the temperature now feels comfortable. Again she fears that I will take her leaving the hour as terrible. I remind her that the wish to do so came up at the beginning of the analysis and that she has at last acted on it. She says it is better to talk. I say she acts first and talks later, characteristically, but she hasn't yet talked as much as she needs to. She speaks of her inhibitions, and I point out that her experience today tells us of strong wishes that she inhibits.

On the following day she returns, saying it is harder and harder to talk. It took a lot of courage, she feels, to get the water. She seeks my approval again, and I comment on that. Then she recognizes that we still don't know what it meant, and I agree. She thinks of reading about fellatio and about wetness in the vagina and of her boyfriend's wish to be a father. She tells a dream:

> I am at a house with three sides surrounded by shrubbery but open on the fourth. How can I sunbathe so exposed? My father says it is too expensive to plant more shrubbery.

She thinks of shrubbery on people's bodies. Then she returns to yesterday's hour: "It was different from any other." She had wanted to breathe fresh air, and she felt freer. Again she worries about my reaction. I point out that she has drawn her own attention to a connection between inhibition and unconscious wishes. She wonders about her wish for approval. Is it because of her own disapproval? I ask her what the word "shrubbery" might bring to mind. "Scrubbing and bathtubs—rubbing—masturbation and being rubbed! You knew!" I acknowledge that I did, and I point out the three-sided enclosure of the shower represented in the dream and the condensation of shower and rub in shrubbery. I suggest that a childhood wish to take her father's penis in her mouth to make a baby is revived in the analysis, as she thinks of getting married and having a baby. This leads to the pressure to get out of the analytic session, away from that wish, away from my penis, but also to drink the water to gratify the wish symbolically. She is noticeably less anxious for the remainder of the session as she reviews past and present experiences and as she remembers the sexual excitement of father's drying her body, pressing on her clitoris. She feels he should have stopped, and she wonders what had been in it for him and why mother allowed it.

In this transference reaction, memory, stimulated by present wish and fantasy, dominates the free associations, just breaching the rule of verbal expression in the acting out of getting the glass of water. This is an example of the disruptive tendency outlined in the third part of my definition of transference. I am speaking here of transference *as* resistance, not of resistance against the expression of transference. The action of getting the glass of water disrupts the agreement for anaylsis through the *form* of association. Characteristically, in transference reactions the patient seeks direct gratification in fulfillment of wishes and relief from anxiety, whether in action, as in the present instance, or within the verbal sphere. The conscious attitudes induced by transference motivations tend to supersede the agreement for *free* association; that is, for association free of conscious direction. The analyst's interventions, especially interpretation, serve to restore the original agreement and to promote greater freedom of association.

The transference, in this example, appears to be highly specific in its re-creation of the memory of the childhood fellatio fantasy. Relief of tension came when I directed her attention to the meaning of "shrubbery." She felt understood and understood herself. To my ear the precise effect of transferred memory operates here to a greater extent than was the case in the third month of her analysis, where tension generally aroused played a significant part.

It was more than another year later, in a phase of mother transference, that she dreamed that her neighbor, a woman of her mother's age, invited the patient to see *her* husband's beautiful bathroom shower. This dream was immediately followed by a political diatribe against me for my supposed opposition to women's rights. We understood this as an expression of resentment to her mother, both for rejection, in being sent off to an intolerable relationship with her father, and for defeat in competition, which now found separate expression.

Such successive, intense transference reactions are the stuff of which the transference neurosis is made. The analyst seems always to be in the center of the patient's attention, and the analysis travels from transference to transference, as one memory after another comes to dominate the free associations. But transference does not always play such a central role, and memory does not always etch its form so sharply on the free associations. My own experience is in agreement with views expressed by Greenacre (1959) in regard to the variable texture of the "so-called transference neurosis." In any event, as is the case for all aspects of free association, the role of transference differs from patient to patient and from phase to phase in each analysis.

The tendency to develop transference reactions, as noted at the beginning of this chapter, is not created by analysis. Much of analysis involves the clarification of transference reactions in the patient's current relationships outside analysis. Just as I do not find it useful to think of the fundamental tendency to develop relationships as transference, I do not assume that the ordinary elements of personal choice necessarily operate on the basis of unconscious memory. On the other hand, when a husband takes his wife's sexual inhibition as the repetition of his mother's withdrawal into depression, or when a mother takes her two-year-old son's obstinacy as though it were angry rejection by her father, the concept of transference is relevant. For in these circumstances an unconscious memory operates to re-create an old relationship and tends to disrupt the relationship on which it is imposed.

The useful designation of the transference as positive and negative is naturally a heuristic fiction, in which we look at relationships from the viewpoint of ambivalence. No small component of human nature, ambivalence is, however, only one aspect by which the transferences can be grouped. We classify the transferences also according to the developmental phase of the memory involved, according to the conflicts which may be related, and according to the person, especially the figures of childhood, with whom the original relationship was experienced. And, as for other aspects of free association, classifications can be formulated as the occasion arises.

Perhaps more than in any other aspect of free association,

analysts vary in their temperamental and theoretical proclivities when it comes to the analysis of transference. The free
association method requires of the analyst a willingness to be
involved to some extent in the irrational drama of the transference. This requirement is both a challenge, on which analysts
and analysis thrive, and a chore, for transference exerts a tension between adult experience and childhood experience, between adult thinking and childhood thinking, between adult
aims and childhood aims, on the analyst as well as on the patient. The analyst must find a means to combine the experience
of transference with a capacity to sustain his own sense of reality and his intention to assist the patient to enhance the free
associations. It seems likely that analysts vary in regard to
styles of management and modes of formulation not only one
from another but from one kind of transference to another, from
patient to patient, and even from time to time in the course of
their lives. In addition to developing one's own synthesis of
psychoanalytic observation, formulations, and technique,
each analyst must, of course, also develop those personal aspects of temperament that facilitate the experience and management of transference. The usefulness of a definition of transference in terms of free association may be extended if the concept of countertransference is defined in comparable ways. In
such a conception the determinants of the analyst's associations would form the basis of the definition.

10

Illustrations of the Free Association Process

Psychoanalysts naturally think of treatment as a process or, more accurately, as a number of parallel processes. Such a concept of process aims to correlate the course of the analysis with a formulation of the patient's disorder and with the relatively slow evolution of the modifications and changes achieved. In this chapter I discuss some important components of the psychoanalytic process, which I define as the free association process, that is, as the outcome of the systematic use of the free association method. In defining the process in this way I do not preclude other formulations, based on theoretical concepts. On the contrary, my hope is that others may find it useful to coordinate the theoretical formulations of their preference with these formulations in terms of the method of free association (Blum, 1976; Dewald, 1978; Loewald, 1980; Ritvo, 1978).

When I speak of the free association process I have in mind two parallel and complementary descriptive aspects. The first has received more attention throughout the preceding chapters, and, in a sense, it has been their subject. It starts with the idea of the therapeutic functions of free association in analysis, whose effects are to promote continuities and to increase the freedom of association. In several examples I have indicated some of the dimensions of change that measure such effects, suited to the individual analysis. I shall not review them here. In all, they provide an external view of the process, in which the interrelationships of its parallel components can be assessed. Formulations of how the method of free association produces its effects derive from this aspect of process. It is, in that sense, a higher order of formulation than the concept of the functions of free association. It is based on patterns in segments of analysis rather than on sequences within hours. Process also implies the complexity of the conditions that are treated with analysis. I find it useful to picture the mental elements of psychopathology joined to one another in obligatory condensation, intertwined and inseparable under ordinary circumstances. Free association provides the means for gradual loosening of the bonds, that is, for analysis in the specific sense of separating out the elements.

The second descriptive aspect of the process of free association emphasizes the experience of its participants. In one way, of course, analysis is the investigation and increasing awareness of the patient's experience. Attention does not usually focus, however, on the experience of the process, that is, on how the patient experiences the analysis. Patients often comment on it, but they do so selectively, and the expansion of association in this direction is not generally in the patient's interest. One common exception to this rule relates to the rhythm of analysis. Patients often note the sense of interruption when hours must be missed, a sense that cannot be wholly attributed to meanings based on transference and other unconscious attitudes to the analyst or to the urgency of therapeutic need. An induced pressure for free association and the sense of continuity and rhythm are intrinsic elements of the free association process.

Analysts, unlike patients in this regard, are keenly interested in the experience of the analytic process. So, here, it is the analyst's associations that I depend upon to describe the feel and texture of analysis. When the treatment starts we usually know very little of the patient, even after several consultation sessions. Yet at first we know where we are, in one way, for we are at the beginning, and the patient is there, too. Conscious and preconscious influences on the free associations dominate their thrust. Just as surely, but surprisingly nonetheless, we are soon traveling in uncharted waters, on course only insofar as the method of free association is applicable and so long as we hold to it. As unconscious influences increasingly dominate the free associations, and as the transferences appear, breaking at times like storms upon our ship, the whole voyage of analysis seems to have a life of its own: not out of control, but not controlled by us or by our patient. Ineffable, perhaps, and always with a special feel of its own, this aspect of process is an essential characteristic of psychoanalysis. I have this aspect always in mind, although formulation of the process according to the parallel external view of the functions of free association and their effects comes more readily to hand, at least, for me.

In speaking of these two aspects of process, I touch upon a feature of the method of free association that I did not discuss earlier: the frequent shifts of attention required of both analyst and patient. The free association method allows no mechanical application of principles. Experiential and observational perspectives interdigitate with formulative and with reflective ones. Patients clearly vary in these perspectives; so do analysts, no doubt.

I agree entirely with the view often expressed that the analyst must interrupt free association to enhance it or that the question of what constitutes enhancement of the free associations has, at best, only a subjective answer—subject, that is, to the patient's judgment, ultimately. I am suggesting, in fact, that such a view does not go far enough, for patient and analyst must allow themselves to be largely ignorant as they make their judgments. They resolve to immerse themselves in uncertainty and ambiguity by following the free association method, relying on the development of a process with intrinsic limits of its own to bring the venture to a sound conclusion. For some patients the balance of terror between the uncertainties of the treatment process and the desperation of the unyielding constraints of psychopathology proves to be the decisive factor. In this sense a "resistance to treatment" may lead to reluctance to pursue free association.

I want to give an example of such an occurrence, where the limits of the method are exceeded. A divorced man in his late forties consulted me on the advice of his internist. A chronic symptom of not being able to urinate in public toilets was driving him crazy, he said. He had been in a variety of treatments, including two attempts at behavioral therapies, over the course of more than 20 years. He was chronically somewhat depressed. Some connections I made between several of his comments, linking recent events with memories from early childhood, suggested to him that I might be able to understand both him and his symptoms. He was especially pleased that I understood a memory of garbage men singing on the street outside his childhood home as a reference to the "music" of early childhood love that he wished to regain. He wanted analysis. My own view was less sanguine, and I urged him to try once more a behavioral approach, after which, with symptomatic pressure reduced, he could make a judgment on whether he really wished to have an analysis. He accepted my referral but after several weeks broke off the behavior therapy, finding his interest more and more in the line of his own development as a person, where limitations from an extremely traumatic childhood showed themselves on all fronts. Diagnostically I could not rule out a borderline psychotic condition, and later I came to believe that it was, in fact, the case. We agreed to try analysis.

From the beginning the patient overvalued my abilities in his extreme idealization. This was so exaggerated at times that it appeared more contrived than genuine on those occasions, and some of his remarks, later, as he grew disappointed, supported this impression. To what extent this idealization represented, exclusively or partially, a transference, that is, the operation of a memory of an early childhood relationship, to what extent it was the expression of a wish, old or new, or the result of externalization of one side of a generally ambivalent and immature characteristic way of relating was hard to determine. We gained rapidly an understanding of a bizarre childhood homelife, with an utterly self-centered mother, who could give him everything so long as he was willing to lie in bed with her, and with a father whom he detested, who hardly spoke words, and who physically beat him very frequently. The crucial event of his childhood was the collapse of his mother, when he was about five years old, into a depressive and psychosomatic illness that kept her largely in bed for the rest of her life. We gained, too, an understanding of many meanings of his symptom of urinary inhibition. Among them were connections with separation from home in going to school, with sexual excitement, and with the beatings. His mood improved greatly over several months. From depression and desperation he moved toward optimism, which was quite different from remembered experiences of elation and hypomania and from one brief episode on the edge of megalomanic delusion, several years earlier. His relationships at work, with friends, and with his children gained noticeably.

All this improvement was followed, after several months, by hints of reluctance to continue analysis. First came conflicts over whether he could afford the fee, then complaints that he was not getting from me what he needed, namely, a "real" relationship, even one confined to the scheduled sessions, in which he could experience my warmth and friendliness. Gradually, he became depressed again. We were able to link his disappointment in me with his much earlier disappointment in his mother. He wanted a loving relationship with me, which he recognized as an attempt to remake the past. The mutuality of our purpose, the therapeutic alliance, remained strong, although the understanding we gained had little influence. What interfered, I believe, was not my refusal to respond to his wishes, for he was able to recognize my continuing warmth, nor a rejection of me as a reversal of rejection by his mother, turning passive into active. I believe that his inability to gain the satisfaction he needed through the activity of free association determined the outcome. The decisive factors lay in conflicts over hostility to his mother, in guilt for wanting independence, and in the devastation he had suffered when he lost her. These attitudes and memories gained control of the free associations in unyielding conflicts of ambivalence. In his assessment at this time none of the insights that had seemed so fresh and exciting a few months earlier had been new; certainly he found them of no use. A new meaning of his symptom emerged rapidly under these circumstances: to let go, to urinate, was to lose everything, to be empty. He returned for his next session determined to stop the treatment. He was most cordial and remained so in a number of subsequent contacts. I asked why he felt no resentment, and he explained that in his view there was no cause for resentment at me. He supposed that a man who had been beaten as much as he was cannot change.

I believe that here, over a period of several months, the threat of hate, guilt, and utter emptiness in the transference, repeating the traumatic disintegration of his life when his mother became ill, determined the outcome of the analysis. He seems to me to have chosen to abandon the attempt to regain his early love for her rather than to reexperience the traumatic loss when he was five and the much earlier strain trauma of her refusal to accept and to support his growing independence. So far as I could tell, the sadistic treatment that he suffered at his father's hands did not enter the transference. Although he referred to the beatings in terminating, I do not believe he felt beaten by me. Perhaps he meant that had he had a good relationship with his father, he could have trusted the outcome with me when hate in the mother transference threatened to obliterate us both. Reluctance to proceed appeared in the final step, but the process that led to it was gathering momentum over an extended period. Whether he was correct in his certainty that impending transference conditions would prove too painful and would be fruitless to endure, or whether his impression was the result of an overestimation of the unconscious forces at work I cannot say. I have no reason, however, to assume he was incorrect in his decision. He retreated from the threat of hostility and devastating guilt at the expense of hope. Nonetheless, so far as I could determine from our later contacts, there was some lasting improvement from the treatment, incomplete as it was. Guilt did not lead, as it can, to a negative therapeutic reaction.

I turn now to another treatment, in which conditions were more favorable for the analytic process. It provides the opportunity to place in the context of a single treatment successive examples of a variety of forms, functions, and consequences of free association and to indicate the changing quality of therapeutic alliance and mutuality of insight. This will permit me to indicate some dimensions of process that correspond to the patient's psychopathology. While I shall select only a few threads from the tapestry, my aim is to demonstrate the intricacy of the weave that underlies the picture.

An able man in his early thirties, well esteemed for his scholarly work, consulted me on the possibility of undertaking analysis because he suffered from mild chronic depression and because he had little pleasure in his marriage, though he loved his wife and children. He had had two earlier periods of psychotherapy, of which he found the second one helpful. He was dissatisfied with his work, although he was on the brink of advancement and, in fact, gained tenure at the beginning of the second year of analysis. He had always doubted his achievements, but time had severely diminished his earlier faith in his "potential." He complained of forgetfulness, so that he was frequently anxious that his poor memory would lead to some significant oversight, especially at work. When he returned for a second interview he said that he had left my office elated, since I had said he "should" have analysis. In fact, I had said he "could" have analysis, and the difference had been made up by an intense longing, whose halting expression was to become one of the strands of the process of his analysis.

The first year of the analysis revealed the problem he faced not only in the contents of his associations but in their form. He was genuinely interested in analysis, he was ready to consider all the possibilities of motivation and unconscious meaning that analysis encounters, he was willing and able to say his thoughts—in short, he was a most cooperative patient. Affect, however, was strikingly muted, and all motivation was restricted. The wish for me to have said that he "should" have analysis was, in the first place, a wish for emotional excitement and freedom. The process of analysis, from this point of view, was the regaining of excitement, but it was also the revealing of how he came to lose it and how it stayed lost.

Self-criticism appeared from the first. Not a single hour failed to provide him with an opportunity to express negative judgments of his character or of his intelligence or of his worth as a husband or father. Tall, slim, and elegant, he retained an image of himself as an obese, ungainly child, slow and awkward, messy and incompetent, who became an angry, crude, vulgar adolescent, obsessed with sex. He was afraid that sexual wishes would get out of control, as he felt they had been in his adolescence, and that hostile ones would lead to explosions of rage, which happened once in his adolescence and once during the early months of analysis, when he thought a stranger had deliberately knocked down one of his children. Among the measures of the analytic process, changes in his image of himself could be observed, as he came to see himself more and more a man.

In regard to analysis he assumed, despite anything I might say, that I too was critical of him. He always apologized for not remembering dreams well, an example of his symptom of a poor memory, so it represented a breakthrough when, after six months, he told a dream and added that this was the first he remembered readily: a boy wearing a T-shirt with the name of his childhood camp is harassing him; he tells the boy that it isn't nice for a camp M___boy to be doing that. The dream acknowledged the recognition of his self-criticism, but it also expressed a sarcastic imitation of a parental voice—mine, as he experienced it in the analysis—telling him to be "nice." This was the voice of his mother, against whom so much of his muted but abundant anger was directed. This dream and its analysis permitted him to see the externalization of self-criticism and an emerging mother transference in which he experienced my pointing out his self-criticism as one more admonition to be good. His mother, he would say, specialized in force-feeding her family, especially himself, which he enormously resented. He railed against his family's inertia, their lack of hobbies and activities. When he wanted to help his mother cook, she said, "You'll be the biggest help to me if you're a good boy." He saw me in this light. Memory of the dream owed its clarity, I now believe, to the relative freedom to express his hostility to me, in the sarcastic message of the dream.

The patient's father, by far the favorite parent of both the patient and his three-year older brother, had severe rheumatic heart disease from the time the patient was about four years old. He died ten years later. All competitive transferences in the analysis derived from the relationship with his older brother. In our very first contact over the telephone, as I gave the patient directions to my office, he found me "fussy," like a somewhat older colleague who had been trained under the same chief. He had in fact done very little with his father during his childhood, partly because his father did very little more than sit around at home (though he maintained his professional work), partly out of a need to keep his distance from his father. His older brother had been more fortunate, and throughout childhood was envied and admired by the patient for his physical and social abilities. In the year before his father died, the patient went fishing with him—mainly sitting—but at least that much could be counted upon in memory.

From the beginning of the analysis the patient wanted to mourn for his father, for he correctly sensed that his mourning had been incomplete. Among the complications that had intervened, in the year following his father's death, was that his father's business partner had pursued the patient on a number of occasions and, ultimately, succeeded in sexually seducing him. For a very long time the patient wondered why he had allowed it and why, even when his brother later exposed the man for an attempt to seduce him and their mother had barred the man from the house, he had said nothing. He supposed it was because he felt guilty over some homosexual activities with several friends, which had started well before his father's death. After a year of analysis, as the associations were gradually focusing more and more on the lack of "physical magnetism" between him and his wife and on his limited sexual desire, he came upon a new connection. "It occurred to me while cleaning up dog turds that when my wife touches my penis it's like [father's partner] touching my penis." Three days later the patient turned his anger toward me, identifying me with Hitler, in a dream, and with his first, punitive psychotherapist. He complained that a year of treatment had done little for him. I pointed out that these criticisms of me—still muted, but strong, for him—came up in the context of his recalling his father's partner. He returned after the weekend to report a state of euphoria: "All my emotions were sharper, closer to the skin." He had woken up screaming from a dream of driving an ice pick into an inflated plastic toy covered with pictures and symbols of a detested political figure. It had a plastic tube behind its ear—a hearing aid, he thought. The expression of hate in the tranference (the analyst as hearing aid) was connected, here, with the freedom of emotional experience he sought at the beginning of analysis, just as the earlier, sarcastic expression of criticism in the dream of the boy who was harassing him had been connected with clarity of memory.

Several months later, as the summer vacation approached, an extraordinary sequence appeared in the analysis. I have previously (1977) reported the initial fragment of this sequence to illustrate my understanding of "being in a hurry":

The patient regularly and sympathetically reported his wife's frustrations. One of these was her dissatisfaction with the pediatrician of their young children. Since their contact was very frequently limited to telephone consultations, she feared that serious illness might be missed. Accordingly, she wanted to shift their medical insurance coverage to an available prepayment health care plan that many friends had found satisfactory. Although the patient thought it was a good idea, his ensuing associations showed dissatisfaction. It turned out that what bothered him was that in shifting to the prepayment plan he would have to give up his own internist at the university health service, Dr. B., whom he greatly admired and with whom he felt particularly secure.

He began the next hour by saying that I had pointed out to him the day before that analysis could help him know what he wants. He went back to the matter of the health care plan and said, "It makes sense to consider staying with Dr. B." I pointed out that in his usual way he had said "it makes sense," not what he wanted or felt. Somewhat sadly he asked if I understood that it was hard for him to know what his feelings were. I told him I did understand and that that was where free association came in to help. He said with feeling that he could begin to understand that. From there he went to a dream which implied self-criticism because of his lack of sexual interest, and then to the recurrent themes of dangers and death in connection with sexual wishes. There was further elaboration in the next hour. He began the following session, saying, "A lot happened this weekend" and immediately reported a dream:

> I was watching Adam [his son] in the front of an orphanage. My wife and I were dead. A man was going to show him our graves. I saw him skipping down the road, innocent, heartbreakingly charming. My wife and I were missing, but Adam didn't know we were dead.

His first thought on waking up was that the dream took place in the village where his mother was born. He woke up scared. He thought that I was the man and he was Adam and that the dream meant that I would show him that his father was (really) dead. He wondered about the place of mother's birth and said, "She's screwed up." He reported some fears over the weekend that his sister-in-law might have an accident with the car while Adam was with her. His thoughts then turned to the good news: on Saturday afternoon for the second time in their marriage his wife had had an orgasm during intercourse; the lovemaking had been very good. On Sunday she had fondled him in bed in the morning and, overcoming his initial irritation, he had had a sudden surge of sexual desire. He penetrated her, but they had had to stop when they heard Adam get up and open the door of his room. Sunday night they had made love again. He now returned to the dream and to Adam's plight, which had brought tears to his eyes. He wondered about my showing him his father's grave.

I commented on the sequence of sexual satisfaction and the fear of an automobile accident (Sunday) and the dream in which the patient's annoyance with Adam for interrupting the lovemaking had led to a terrible punishment for Adam. He could see that. I wondered whether there was a connection between death and mother's birthplace. "Her genitals," he said immediately. He recalled the prohibition against going into his parents' bedroom, which he took so seriously as a child that once when he awoke at 5 in the morning, vomiting, he did not go in. His mother said that that would have been an exception to the rule. He recalled suspecting some reason for this rule and could now see that the strong wish to enter had led to strong internal countermeasures. He saw the relationship between these thoughts and Adam, as he interrupted them and as he appeared in the dream. Finally, he brought up some dissatisfaction with the cottage he had seen on Sunday that his wife's parents had arranged for him to rent for the summer vacation, 6 weeks later. He was pleased with himself for knowing, for once, what it was that bothered him, but he wondered why he felt dissatisfied [pp. 97–99].

In my earlier publication I noted that in this hour the patient's characteristic tendency to want to leave each session in a hurry, as the hour drew to a close, was absent for the first time in the analysis. I attributed this change to a shift in tolerance of his passive wishes for me at the end of the session. He *expressed* frustration about the summer plans in his associations instead of having to act in hurrying away. I suggested that this change was due to the satisfaction of passive wishes which occurred when he asked if I understood how hard it was for him to know his own feelings and in helping him to see his love for Dr. B. and his wish to continue to be cared for by him. The release of active sexual desire from the usual inhibitions and restrictions to which it was subject followed that gratification and, in turn, I believe, led to the absence of the reaction of hurrying. This seemed to me a typical sequence in the alternation of expression and satisfaction that occurs in the free association process in the case of conflicts of ambivalence. Here the ambivalence was between active and passive libidinal wishes, which had been yoked in obligatory condensation.

The sessions which followed did not retain the excitement of the last one. There was some reviewing of that hour; the alternating themes of fear and desire were prominent; there was again an instance of not making love when he would have wanted to; and at the end of each hour in that week he was in a hurry to leave.

Over the next weekend the patient and his wife discovered that she had a breast lump. An earlier one had been benign. This one, too, appeared to be benign, but the patient did not mention that a mammogram was scheduled for the end of the week. After speaking of some concerns about increasing responsibilities at work, he returned to the topic of their sexual life, which was "looking up." His wife was continuing to have vaginal orgasms; she was now more appealing to him, and there was more "spice" in the lovemaking. He wanted to know more about the connection between sex and death and the dream of being dead in mother's birthplace. He wondered if he had thought that his parents' sex life had led to his father's death. In a film of the black widow spider that he had seen in connection with his work, intercourse means death for the male. He thought of a coming visit to his mother, who would overfeed him as in childhood. His thoughts took him to his former cars in succession; the last, a Triumph, which he gave up in anticipation of getting married. I suggested that the cars he mentioned had often been connected with the development of his sexual life, with its greater vitality before marriage. It seemed that we had to conclude that the black widow spider, mother's birthplace, was connected not only with father's death but with the death of his own penis. To this he responded with interest, with doubt about the permanence of his sexual improvement, and, once again, with an absence of hurrying to leave.

That night the patient had a dream after he felt too tired to make love, though his wife had wanted to:

I was next to a tower by a pool. Perhaps a diving tower. Rachel [his daughter] fell off the tower. I wasn't watching carefully, but she landed sitting and unhurt.

My wife and I were driving through suburban G____, across town from where we live. According to my wife, Mrs. L. had said that that was the best part of G____. We entered T____ [which doesn't actually touch on G____]. We were at the top of a hill, next to the bay (though there is none in T____]. In the best part of G____, the houses were ramshackle.

A disreputable drunk without teeth appeared. I was talking with my wife and realized she had been unfaithful to me with him. He was thirty-seven.

The absurdities in the dream, the impossibility of really getting from G____ to T____, and the best part being ramshackle referred first of all to his views on my interpretation of the cars and the castration theme in the previous hour. That is, he thought it absurd, he didn't know how I arrived at it, and he wasn't impressed by the best I had to offer, i.e., the castration complex. We were both amused by this first meaning of the dream. What bothered him, however, was Rachel's falling and the fear of his wife's infidelity. He recalled that in childhood one of his friends had told him that women had had penises and were castrated. On the basis of many past dreams where water had been connected with his own urinating, in nocturnal enuresis, I suggested that the first part of the dream might be connected with childhood interpretations of why women sit down to urinate and the reassurance that they are unhurt. He could follow that, but why was it his fault? He wondered why he cannot resolve his castration fear.

The following day he acknowledged a further thought that he had not expressed, that he would never resolve the fear. Another matter, however, had taken center stage. A phone call home, during the afternoon after the dream had been reported, had not been answered. He wondered if his wife were unfaithful to him, in fact. She had gone out shopping that night, which increased his worries. Had the dream been a preview? He was terribly upset, and his account was difficult to follow. Thoughts of divorce led to memories of greater sexual pleasure before marriage, impropriety adding spice, like buying liquor before age twenty-one. I reminded him of the drunk in the dream. He was thirty-seven, old looking, and had no teeth. Only to thirty-seven was there an association. A friend at work had had his thirty-seventh birthday a week earlier and talked of life being half over. I pointed out the many themes we had heard of: castration; losing his wife; losing his father; and death. Aware that thirty-seven referred to my street address, I added the coming summer vacation. His immediate association was to the summer cottage he had rented. What dissatisfied him was the fact that it was not directly on the lake, and so he could not get up and go fishing first thing in the morning. I showed him that he was also speaking of the time at which he came for his analytic hour, first thing in the morning. We could now see the wish expressed in going from G___ to T___ in the dream, even though, like our summer vacation places, they were not contiguous. He saw it and suddenly felt "inundated" and "frightened." He said, "I want to hurry away."

Here, as is so often the case, both dreams clearly represent the continuation of free association from the previous session during sleep. Under conditions related to those of the analytic session, but also different from them, an altered balance between thrust and opposition leads to expression of wishes that have remained silent in the presence of the analyst. In the case of the second dream, when the patient has gradually approached those wishes through the associations, aided by my focus on the details of dream construction, my interpretation of the meaning of going from G___ to T___ brings him a cognitive insight that is followed by a strong affective response. Such reactions occur regularly as concomitants of the expansion of free association and are an important part of the free association process.

To return to the narrative of the prevacation sequence: the intense emotion at the end of the last session did not entirely abate. The patient began the next session with considerable agitation. All weekend long he had had a horrible fear of his wife's being unfaithful, though he knew it was neurotic. I pointed out that we needed to understand the unconscious meaning of his doubts, which came up as a consequence of his attempt to get to know his shut-off feelings. Then he said that his wife had had a mammogram on Friday, which showed the lump to be benign, though it was to be watched. He suggested that he might have been afraid of losing his wife through breast cancer. I told him that I had not been aware of the planned mammogram, but now it seemed likely that some fears about the harmfulness of his sexual practice of kissing and sucking on his wife's breasts might be connected with the toothless drunk of the dream. His thoughts took him back to their wedding night. They had tried to make love, but her thick hymen had made penetration extremely painful to her. I suggested (as I had on earlier occasions) that the pain he caused her had influenced the decline in his sexual interest in her. I emphasized again the fear of his own aggressiveness. He suggested hostility as a possible source of his doubts. In his great anxiety he wondered what to do, what to tell his wife, because she justly complained that he was so preoccupied with himself that he failed to pay attention to her anxiety. I suggested that he might tell her that it is hard to be the wife of a man in analysis. (This "suggestion" was a step toward the clarification of the transference meaning of his doubts.) He went on to say that they had again made love three times, but twice he had had trouble keeping his erection. I suggested that this might be due to an unconscious fear of the repetition of the wedding night. I related it to his dream of two weeks earlier, where he and his wife were dead, in contrast to the current return of feeling and increased lovemaking.

By the next day he was a great deal calmer, the fear of his wife's infidelity markedly lessened. He debated whether he should tell her about it, though he thought it was probably better not to. I wondered whether he might not wait to tell her at least until he knew more of its meaning. That agreed with his instinctive feeling. She would think he was a nut, verging on insanity. He went on to connect this with bedwetting. Was it hostile to his mother, he mused.

In the following session he pursued the theme of his own inadequate sexual performance. Even with the girls he had been successful with prior to marriage he was sometimes impotent. One occasion in particular was the first time he made love to a girl in his mother's and stepfather's new house, in a glassed-in porch. He now reviewed some matters that had come up during the course of the analysis. He recalled the many months in which we had studied his anger in the first year of analysis. "I got bored with anger," he said. "I thought it was your game, not mine. Now I believe anger is connected with sex." He wondered about his doubt: hurting his wife or loving her. His thoughts went back to the girls before marriage; always the fear of getting caught. The end of the hour approached, and he glanced furtively at the clock for an instant. I suggested that time and doubt may be connected, perhaps something about not getting caught.

In the next hour there was a dream:

> My wife and I were in her parents' cottage, at the windows, which were in a sawtooth pattern. I saw a path outside from the right side. Some adolescent boys came by and caught sight of us, of my wife. They looked in. Then, to my relief, they moved on.

Rachel had been ill with a fever last night; she saw things coming at her. His wife had spent the night with her in the guest room. The thoughts of infidelity were coming back. While thinking of making love with his wife, he had an image of teeth clamped on his penis. He imagined ice tongs clamped on his head, and he complained that he had had very few chances to see those tongs in use—a few times in the summers of his childhood. He remembered seeing a turtle eat a fish. He wondered whether there was a connection with fears for his penis. I suggested that he might want to notice his emphasis on looking. The sawtooth pattern led to a new building with its windows that way. One had already been smashed. Yesterday he wondered if he should go to the bathroom here. Two or three times a few months ago he had suddenly had to urinate on the way to work, after his session. He had raced to the bathroom there. He again suggested a connection between hostility, urination and bedwetting.

After the weekend the patient reported some mild, vague uneasiness. The lovemaking was good, again, but now his wife and children were away for two days at her parents' house. He came to the thought of my vacation and then to a dream of which he remembered only that it was about a particular colleague. (This was the fussy, obsessive, long-winded man who had been a regular stand-in for me on innumerable occasions from the very beginning.) The man had returned yesterday from vacation. They had had a gratifyingly short conversation. I suggested that he wanted me to have a gratifyingly short vacation. As he reviewed his feelings, he said, "I feel more in touch with my body for the last two weeks." But despite feeling better he had been withdrawn on Saturday. Muted expressions about a close friend at work leaving gave me the opportunity to connect his uneasiness to the unexpressed feelings about my vacation. He wondered if the doubts about his wife were similar.

On the following day after speaking of several matters at work he came upon a thought he did not want to tell. The day he had made the telephone call to his wife that had led to the fear of her infidelity, he had seen a patient of mine in passing, as he was leaving a meeting. He had noted that this man shared a characteristic with him and with his father. I said that this encounter must be the source of the fear of infidelity. He asked, "Do you mean that I felt you were unfaithful to me in seeing other patients?" Ridiculous, he thought. I ventured a suggestion that unconscious meanings be given some attention. His associations led him to denigrate two other men whom he then connected with my other patient. He began to realize that unconsciously the vacation was like a childhood separation from mother. Now he recalled that the telephone call he made to his wife came half an hour after seeing my other patient. He also recalled that he had been on the way to the toilet to urinate when he saw him. Rapidly he gained a sense of conviction about the transference meaning of his fear of his wife's infidelity. There was a subdued state of amazement and a sense of relief. The transference meanings were elaborated over subsequent sessions to include the sense of his mother's infidelity to him with his father and his own infidelity to his wife in the analysis. He recalled being told that when he was a small child, around four, his parents left for a trip of several weeks, returning to find him ill. A slight doubt lingered on. Two weeks later, in the sessions just before the vacation, the associations brought into focus the annual separation from father, who would remain in town while the rest of the family went on vacation, joining them only on weekends for the first part of the summer. He recalled again how much he enjoyed going fishing with him.

This intense sequence of sessions, occurring in a period of six weeks, allows for any number of emphases and formulations. For present purposes, the interplay of transferences and realities, past and present influences on the associations, the action of a variety of wishes and anxieties from different eras of his development, the operation of conflicts of defense side by side with conflicts of ambivalence, and the role of free association in unraveling the tangled skein of neurosis are readily discerned. There was no way that patient or analyst could know exactly—then, or even now—what was taking place. There was no doubt, however, that a great deal was happening as freedom of thought and feeling replaced restriction.

This powerful experience was, nonetheless, far from bringing the analysis to a successful conclusion. The analysis, in fact, required several additional years. Many of the themes adumbrated in this sequence were gradually expanded. I shall take up only a few of these in order to illustrate further the intricate organization of neurosis and its analysis.

On his return from the summer vacation, the patient was once again grimly depressed. There was no excitement anywhere. Gradually, over three months, the analysis came back to life. He became angry and then sexually aroused, with an emphasis on looking. Three months more brought an important memory. In the house that the patient had lived in until he was four years old, his parents had cut a hole into the wall between their bedroom and his closet, in order to hear him, as an infant. A few weeks later a dream of smelts in tomato sauce proved to refer to smelly, black women's genitals and to menstruation. Linked to two cleaning women of his childhood, one of them frightening to him, this dream indicated childhood knowledge and fears. The summer separation, the third of the analysis, brought the most important insight and a clarification. The trip that his parents had taken, that he referred to a year earlier, was not when he was around age four but before he was three. It turned out that his mother had fallen ill with pneumonia when the patient was two years and four months of age. Her illness was followed by a period of some sort of depression, after which both parents took a three-week trip. They returned to find the patient severely ill with pneumonia. He was then about two years and nine months old.

It appeared to us, and much supporting evidence followed, that the swings of emotion in the transference and the search for excitement with which the patient began the treatment took their origins from an early good relationship with his mother that was disastrously interrupted in his third year of life. We pictured him looking at his mother in bed through the hole in his closet wall or wanting to do so. We assumed, further, that later looking, motivated by sexual curiosity, had become condensed with the earlier, restitutive looking. His whole approach to life, we concluded, had been colored permanently by the loss of his mother for such a long period so early in life, imbuing every experience with a threat of frustration, disappointment, and even catastrophe. He could not sustain optimism against the ordinary adversities of life and the internal tides of pessimism to which he remained subject. The sequence of hours from the previous year's prevacation period gained new meaning for us.

Innumerable dreams of restaurants and a like number of dreams of doors and windows opening and closing worked and reworked these problems of loss and of sexual curiosity and fears in the subsequent years of analysis. The opening and closing referred equally to the relationship to his mother and to his own body—to the experience of excitement and depression in relation to both. Only with the closing of the analytic restaurant, however, after six years of analysis, did the transference clarify for us another aspect of the childhood problem of anger at his mother. It turned out that he had concluded as a child that his anger had been responsible for her illness. This conclusion had contributed significantly to the inhibition of aggressive impulses and had played a major role in his relationship with his wife.

In the fourth year of analysis the patient began a session with a dream reminiscent of the one from the prevacation sequence, in which Rachel had fallen from a diving tower by the pool (p. 83):

> I was climbing a ladder, next to a ship's bunk beds. I had things in my hands and couldn't do something I was supposed to—possibly to get into the bunk. I dropped what I had in my hands. The metal frames were painted white— hospital white and sanitary.

Initially his associations ran to lovemaking and to sexual fantasies, then to the problem of withholding, retentiveness, that had come up in the previous session (which appeared in the dream as "something in my hands"). He spoke of a feeling of precariousness in his position at work and the fear of incompetence ("I couldn't do what I was supposed to do" and "I dropped what I had in my hands"). He then recalled that Adam was about to get his first bicycle from his grandparents. This reminded him of his own first two-wheeler, also at age six. His father had been with him, and he had run into a telephone pole. There had been a large black and blue spot above his penis, where the handlebar had hit ("I dropped what I had in my hands" and "I couldn't do what I was supposed to do," reverting to self-criticism for childhood incompetence and, probably, masturbation). He remembered his embarrassment when his mother wanted him to show the spot to his friend's mother, who was visiting. His thoughts went to Rachel, two years younger than Adam, who would be jealous of Adam's bicycle. She was less timid than Adam, more adventurous. She had been climbing the railing on the porch, six feet above the ground. He had told her not to screw up his new paint job, but he hadn't worried about her hurting herself. I asked the color of the paint. White, he said, and I drew his attention to the dream. He had thought of the difference between Rachel's gutsiness and his own timidity. He recalled his fears of getting hurt in boxing with his older brother. Then he remembered jumping out of a tree at age six, breaking his foot. He was in a cast (hospital white) all summer and couldn't go in the water! He had wanted to be held upside down to get in, but his father's bad heart had foreclosed even that possibility.

The second dream permits additional retrospective analysis of the first. There, in context of the earlier dream of being dead in mother's birthplace and subsequent associations, it was possible to guess that falling unhurt into water could be connected with questions from childhood of whether women's genitals result from loss of a penis. In view of many references that had related water with urination and bedwetting it seemed plausible that the image referred to the fact, which makes such an impression on children, that women sit to urinate while men can stand. Additional meanings, it now turns out, are to be found in fears of injury connected with his own fall, which is futher related to a groin injury and to his mother's insensitivity to his feelings in having him show the black and blue spot to her friend. The child falling into the water, surprisingly, appears now to recall the childhood wish to be held upside down by his father. I wonder if this represents, in the adult dream, a wish for his analyst, as a healthy father, to help him fulfill his wishes.

In these two dreams, more than two years apart, the links between illness and injury can be seen again and again. Death and disease are always on his mind, and, it appears, always have been. Every developmental phase and achievement, it seems, has been colored by such thoughts. The reality of both his father's and his mother's illnesses, and illnesses and injuries of his own and of his wife's contributed significantly to the entrenchment of his neurosis.

I shall close this account with an aspect of our understanding of the patient's relationship with his father. We had been puzzled from the beginning by two unexplained matters. First, the patient felt he had been unable to complete his mourning for his father. Second, although he preferred his father to his mother and regarded him as more sympathetic to little boys than his mother was and although his father was present at home and friendly to him, during the patient's childhood, the patient remembered very little that they had done together. There were, after all, many nonstrenuous activities that they could have engaged in. It seemed to us that fears connected with father's illness, limitations imposed on aggressiveness toward him, and parallels drawn in childhood between loss of mother and the potential of losing father did not fully account for the picture as we saw it. At the end of the fourth year of analysis a memory unexpectedly clarified a great many earlier associations. As the analysis of retentiveness and withholding proceeded, an intense anal preoccupation dominated the associations. In this context, the patient recalled his father's habit of sitting on the toilet with the door open for long periods of time, so that the patient would frequently observe him. This added another important form of looking to those we had known of earlier. It linked the patient's extensive anal interests with the homosexual ones that had been such a source of concern to him. We were now able to understand that conflicts over his strong attraction to his father's penis, seen through the door of the bathroom, led him to withdraw from his father early in childhood. Later, when he was about eleven years old, they led to his homosexual activities. The most powerful image derived from the adolescent experiences was of observing two other boys engaged in fellatio. This became the basis of conscious adolescent sexual fantasy and recurred repeatedly in dreams during the analysis. One of these dreams had appeared during the prevacation sequence (p. 86), where the adolescent boys saw him and his wife, and "then, to my relief, they moved on." In that context, in a night when his wife left his bed to sleep with Rachel, during a state of anxious jealousy whose immediate unconscious basis was a sense of my infidelity to him with another male patient, the reference seems to be a wish that he himself had moved on from homosexual to heterosexual interests.

The memory of father on the toilet also explained the acquiescence in the seduction by his father's partner, which the patient had earlier connected with his homosexual activities. In retrospect we can understand how, three years earlier, he had linked feelings about his father's partner and his wife, while cleaning up dog turds.

We were aware when we terminated the analysis that something of significance in his relationship to his father had still eluded us. Several months after termination, the patient called for an appointment. He rapidly brought together convincing data that his current state of renewed depression occurred in the context of buying a new and better house and of intense anger at a high institutional official. No brother figure this! He wondered at the same time what there could be to talk about, for he sincerely believed that this state of depression showed the whole analysis to have been an utter failure. The hostility to his father had arrived in the transference, at last.

We made short work of this, in fewer than half a dozen sessions. A dream of a banquet table: an empty chair is next to his, and he gazes beyond it at a woman's breast. The empty chair was mine, he understood. The image is a step back from father to mother as well as a step forward from me to his wife. In the next session he told a dream of finding a dog turd on my lawn as he was coming to the office. His own interpretation, which bothered him, was that he was saying that all he got from me was shit. I suggested that we listen to his associations a little further, in view of the importance of shit and its meanings in his analysis. He recalled with embarrassment the thought while driving to see me of taking the dream turd in his mouth. He understood at once that he was speaking of my penis and of his father's. With this insight, which brought temporary embarrassment and then a sense of great relief, we saw more clearly what it was that had forced him away from his father in childhood and had left him frustrated in his wish to identify and compete with his father fully, as a man.

The process of free association in this analysis led, as is evident, to a greatly increased freedom of association. The therapeutic benefit to the patient was substantial. It would be misleading to assume, however, that the account I have given is complete in regard to any aspect, either in describing the patient's problems, or in revealing influential antecedents and circumstances, or in discussing the outcome of his analytic treatment. I have tried, faithfully, to demonstrate the complexity and sequence of the process, indicating a wide range of components that seem to me quite typical of analysis. Here, too, however, the discussion does not aim at completeness. My aim has been to illustrate the texture of the free association process and its relationship to the complexity of the patient's neurosis.

From the concept of the free association process as a group of parallel component processes it is natural to travel further, toward a theory of therapeutic effects. A discussion of cure, however, beyond a description of the functions and process of free association, lies outside the scope of this book. My hope is to have contributed toward facilitating research in that area.

11

Development and Free Association

Among the formulations of psychoanalytic process, those that focus on psychological development (A. Freud, 1965; Jacobson, 1964; Kernberg, 1976; Mahler et al., 1975; Winnicott, 1958, 1965) hold an especially important position. Emphasizing the disorders of development in psychopathology, they view the treatment as an opportunity to revise faulty development and to facilitate resumption of impeded development. The concept of process, with parallel components observed in sequence over time, applies equally to development and to treatment. Some specific aspects of process, in addition, are held in common. For example, in both processes forward movement regularly comes into conflict with a reluctance to proceed. An only child, faced with the arrival of a younger sibling, may be ready to cast aside all those hard-won developmental achievements that distinguish him from the baby, just as the adult patient, in analysis, may suddenly lose interest in free association when it promises to bring unwelcome evidence of inner conflict. Another aspect of process, the specific function of free association in treatment in attaching words to thoughts and feelings that were previously outside the verbal sphere, has its developmental counterpart.

Free association is an important part of ordinary experience (Lewin, 1955, pp. 274–81). From adolescence onward it clearly becomes a vital influence on normal development—for example, in mourning for the past. More than introspection, rumination, reflection, or reminiscence alone, it provides an integrative vehicle for the preservation and extension of continuity in development. To what degree some form of free association is also required in childhood, different at different phases of development, in a way that parallels free association in psychoanalytic treatment seems a question worthy of answer. I have in mind some largely preconscious review of experience, through play, in dreams, and in fantasy, that performs some or all of the functions of adult free association both in analysis and outside it. While I cannot speak from experience in this, I am inclined to believe that useful parallels could be drawn between the process of childhood development and the process of child analysis (Ritvo, 1978). As is usual in such considerations, the manner of stating the question, the way in which developmental process and treatment process are to be compared, is likely to be the most difficult part of the problem. I do not mean to suggest that some simple transposition from consideration of processes in adulthood to those in childhood will suffice.

This question brings me to a topic which I omitted from my discussion of the varieties of free association in chapter 2 in order to expedite my presentation of the elements of the free association method. Developmental influences on the form and content of free association must also be taken into account. The field of child analysis and the various forms of child therapy pay daily tribute to the child's very different orientation to the use of words and to the treatment setting from the adult analytic patient's willingness to suspend ordinary modes of interaction in favor of the free association method. Nor is the treatment of children uniform in this regard across the wide developmental expanse from early childhood into adolescence. On the contrary, the cumulative acquisition of significance of speech and thought throughout childhood development plainly casts its influence on child therapy at different phases. This influence does not come to rest at the borders of adulthood.

It seems to me that older patients—and this may apply to analysts as well—can generally confine experience more readily than can younger ones to the verbal range in which the free association method operates best. The ability to set action aside or, at least, to postpone it comes more naturally in the fifties than in the twenties, although the pressure of transference demands may be indistinguishably preemptive and the belief in transference distortions as great in both.

Such observations apply over a relatively wide range of important components of free association. Memory and fantasy, for example, hold a different significance over the course of adult development (for which I use age as a rough but serviceable indicator). For the young man, in his twenties, the still unsettled need to leave his childhood behind may color memory with a negative hue to render it less attractive. The older man, disappointed in the present, may welcome memories of love and satisfaction to reassure himself that he is capable of loving or worthy of being loved. He will, at any rate, be less threatened by them.

From another perspective, free association in adolescence and for some time thereafter is characteristically dominated by conflicts of ambivalence. These include conflicts among various aspects of loving, between independence and dependence, between indulgence and asceticism, body and intellect, fantasy and reality, and so on. It is helpful to both participants in the free association process to be aware of such age-specific proclivities in following the free associations.

Another powerful and complicated kind of influence that depends on development but becomes an independent factor results from the choices of education, training, line of work, marital partner, and geographic location. While, perhaps, none of these is irrevocable, the external influences exerted on the free association process by their consequences are often substantial and sometimes decisive. The fear of many married patients that analysis may wreck their marriage is far from idle. It is the fortunate case when such fears prove to be based mainly on the expectation that the analyst may hear only the negative side of an ambivalent attitude to a marital partner. It is far harder when analysis brings a patient to a point of wanting more than that marriage can offer. Reluctance in the free association process in those circumstances must be sharply distinguished from resistance.

Such influences, fortunately, play an impartial role and can also have a salutary effect on the analytic process. For example, the patient who graduates from a training program, free from the role of student at last, may be far more able to withstand some embarrassments and humiliations of free association. Marriage may provide a variety of supports to facilitate the analytic process. For example, it may quiet homosexual anxieties sufficiently to allow their analysis. It can do the same for loneliness. And parenthood and other new responsibilities may provide an impetus for mastery of immature reactions and old, unsettled conflicts.

I have raised these issues for further exploration. My aim in this addendum has been to emphasize an additional influence on analytic work: the developmental context of free association.

12

Free Association in Psychotherapy

In describing the elements, the method, the determining influences, and the process of free association, I have bypassed, for the most part, the other components of the psychoanalytic situation (Stone, 1961). I want to consider their facilitating influence on free association as a means of defining the frontier between psychoanalysis and the most closely related form of psychotherapy. My premise holds that at that imaginary line of demarcation psychotherapy is fundamentally similar to psychoanalysis in its emphasis on free association, in its requirements of the therapist for neutrality and anonymity, and in its attention to the therapeutic process. Psychoanalytic psychotherapy is not, in my view, psychoanalysis *manqué*, however, for if one crosses the frontier by withdrawing or by altering one of the essential components of the psychoanalytic setting, one must add something else in order to promote the therapeutic process.

Before proceeding with such a functional consideration of some components of the psychoanalytic setting, I want to enter a disclaimer. I do not propose to discuss the many problems that arise when one seeks to clarify the relationship of psychoanalysis to the vast field of psychotherapy, which encompasses a very wide range of methods and circumstances. Nor shall I review the complicated history of the relationship between psychoanalysis and psychotherapy. Sachs (1979) has lately done so most effectively, with a salutary emphasis on Freud's free association method. I am indebted to him for providing such a valuable discussion. I concur with his conclusion that an understanding of the relationship between psychoanalysis and psychotherapy requires distinctions in terms of method.

Accordingly, I shall consider only that segment of the field in which the free association method is the central element of technique. Narrow in that way, it is nonetheless applicable across a wide range of conditions and diagnostic categories, for patients who wish to make use of this kind of treatment.

The two components of the analytic setting whose influence on the free association method I aim to evaluate are (1) the frequent sessions and (2) the use of the couch, with the analyst out of view. I take for granted certain other important features of the analytic setting, such as confidentiality, reasonable quiet, and sessions of sufficient length, which custom has set at fifty minutes.

Psychoanalysis is ordinarily practiced with four or five weekly sessions. So far as I have been able to observe, five weekly sessions are easier on the patient than four. If the frequency of sessions is diminished further, the strain on the patient grows measurably. To understand the significance of frequent sessions and the influence of the patient's expectation of returning again on the following day in inducing and sustaining the thrust of free association, it is necessary to understand the source of strain in diminished frequency. Such strain is often evident in the last session of the week in analysis, when the sense of interruption enters the free associations. While transference reactions and other unconscious attitudes and expectations directed toward the analyst play a role at times in these expressions, they regularly reflect a sense of interruption of the rhythm of the process, to which I referred in chapter 10. The patient expects to miss the process itself.

In less frequent psychotherapy it is the rule rather than the exception that there is an interval of two days or more between sessions, in addition to the usual weekend break. While this repeated sense of interruption does not necessarily interfere with all components of the free association process, such as intensity of transference wishes, for example, it always affects the sense of continuity and rhythm. There is a strain, then, in the conflict between the need to continue free association induced by the free association method and the need to diminish tension in the interval between sessions. For the patient in less frequent psychotherapy this strain usually results in a tendency to diminish the significance of free association. There is a corresponding tendency to substitute formulation for experience, closure for uncertainty. In these circumstances, in order to promote a therapeutic process, the therapist must assist the patient to make formulation and understanding substitute for some of the functions of free association, especially for those that derive from the *activity* of free association rather than from its content. The experience of satisfaction in free association tends to play a lesser role in psychotherapy. This serves additionally to create a therapeutic process different in quality from the free association process in psychoanalysis.

The difference between the process in psychotherapy and the free association process in psychoanalysis is not likely to be evident if one compares a single session or individual components of the therapeutic process, such as recognition of inner conflict or recovery of memory. As Rangell (1954) noted, however, it is in the combination of components, in the texture of the process, that one recognizes the difference. In describing the difference between greater and lesser frequency of sessions in this way, I have stayed deliberately in the realm of the subjective. I shall have to admit that it is even the vague subjective, for who is to tell in a given instance whether the quality of experience is all it could be? On this point, however, patients express themselves clearly. In a large enough number of instances the effects of a shift in frequency, without other changes, have persuaded me of the strain on the patient to maintain the continuity of free association between separated sessions. Patients after analysis can sometimes exert sufficient effort to do so, and in a number of instances I have found once-a-week treatment then to be sufficient for the patient to allow the free associations to lead. Here is the exception that proves the rule, it seems to me, for analysis in these instances had already achieved a result that contributed to the capacity to sustain free association.

The frontier between psychotherapy and psychoanalysis in regard to frequency of sessions is, naturally, open, and patients cross it in either direction and return again. The effects on both sides of the border are cumulative. The patient who enters analysis after a period of psychotherapy does not start at the very beginning. On the contrary, to begin with less frequent sessions may be just right. For some patients to begin the treatment at four or five weekly sessions may be unproductive or harmful. Their needs at that time may not be well served by such intensity of contact or by giving free association primacy. For them, closure and an emphasis on limited insight at first may assist during a troubled period of development, or in times of impending disorganization, or under circumstances where attention is so urgently needed in regard to external matters that the patient would find unlimited free association a source of conflict rather than a means of resolving it.

On the other side, the process in psychotherapy, no matter how diligently and creatively pursued, may reach an asymptotic limit below the level of therapeutic effect that the patient seeks. Sometimes the increase in frequency of sessions leads to a just sufficient quantitative difference as well as to the qualitative one that I have described.

The step between the chair and the couch, the other means of crossing the frontier that I wish to consider, is, like the shift in frequency of sessions, far from absolute. The effects on the free association method of the use of the couch are well known, starting with the evident emphasis it places on verbalization. This applies even more to the analyst's part than to the patient's, because communication of the analyst's nonverbal expressions to the patient is markedly diminished. For the patient whose capacity to express thought and feeling sufficiently in words is limited, the loss of facial expression and bodily gesture as means of communication may interfere with free association rather than enhance it. On the positive side there is a tendency to diminish conscious control of the associations more readily, to increase self-observation, and to emphasize fantasy rather than reality with absence of visual cues. The use of the couch ultimately contributes to the patient's relaxation, though at first it may promote anxiety, and for patients who move from chair to couch it regularly produces an initial sense of loss of the analyst. For the analyst it provides an immediate source of relaxation, which permits greater attention to the free associations. This relaxation results partly from being in a position to allow his facial expressions the free play they need as an intrinsic component of his emotional experience. In addition, the analyst out of view can respond when response is needed but can more readily listen, unguarded against sudden powerfully appealing demands for intervention communicated in facial expressions.

These consequences of the use of the couch are parallel and complementary to those associated with increased frequency of sessions. Taken together they make it more possible to allow the patient's free associations to lead the treatment in psychoanalysis. Conversely, in psychotherapy the vis-à-vis position combined with less frequent sessions permits a greater sense of external organization in the treatment and the substitution of formulation for some actions of free association in the treatment process. The patient in analysis, for example, has a greater likelihood of achieving an identification "with the *functions* of the analyst," in Hoffer's felicitous expression (1950), rather than with the analyst himself.

The use of the couch, like the frequency of sessions, may be adopted or relinquished at times in the course of a patient's treatment, depending on inner and outer circumstances. Again, in my experience, treatment on both sides of the frontier is cumulative.

I have approached the relationship between psychotherapy and psychoanalysis from the viewpoint of the method of free association. In that segment of the field which I have considered, differences in goals are not significant. On neither side of the frontier does the day-to-day therapeutic experience generally bear a readily definable relationship to the patient's goals. The analyst's goals are the same in both: to assist the patient in enhancing his free associations.

13

Prospects for Education and Research

The challenge of mastering the psychoanalytic method requires a formidable investment of self-examination in the analyst's own analysis and in subsequent continuing self-analysis. I have taken this for granted in describing the analyst's role in the free association method. As in every other clinical specialty, training requires supervision of clinical work over a period of years. These two important aspects of the program for training psychoanalysts fall outside the province of this book. The subject that I wish to address here belongs to the third major component of analytic education: the role of theory. How do analysts develop a theoretical approach, and how do they modify it?

In this description of the outlines of the free association method and process in what I believe to be relatively operational terms, aware that I include subjective components in that exposition, my aim has been to permit individual analysts to examine the role of theory, explicit and implicit, in their practice. It seems plausible to me that those who are developing their mastery of the psychoanalytic method might find such an operational approach a useful guide while choosing the theoretical concepts that they will bring to their assistance. This approach could facilitate the process of learning in two ways. First, it could focus attention on the need for formulation as it arises in the clinical situation, where data accumulate in ever greater quantities that require conceptual organization. Second, it could diminish the need to learn a theory out of context. From the point of view of the clinical situation, it is only theory in context, the personal eclecticism of the analyst applied to the large and varied universe of psychoanalytic formulations, that counts in the analyst's hour of need.

Here, I believe, is an essential place for research. We need to know more about the individual styles of conceptualizing and theorizing as they determine the analyst's participation in the free association method. For it seems far from clear to me what makes one way of formulating appeal to one analyst but not to another. Such differences are hard to study when the analytic method and process are defined in terms of the very theoretical concepts in question. A more operational definition of psychoanalytic method and process, such as the one I have offered, seems an essential prerequisite to resolving the present confusion of theoretical tongues.

I do not know whether the approach which I have presented fulfills the requirements for learning and research that I have outlined. It describes as closely as I have been able to formulate it the way that I practice psychoanalysis, leaving aside, however, all but a few of the theoretical formulations that I use in implementing the free association method. It may be that here or there what I take for operational may represent some theoretical predilection of which I am unaware, and others may need to modify the model accordingly.

I do, of course, find theoretical formulations indispensable in my work. My relatively operational approach to the clinical situation allows me to make use of the complex, multidimensional, and still evolving theory that was Freud's second great invention (Friedman, 1978)—the method which is the subject of this book was the first. The structure of Freud's theory differs remarkably from most others in the field, which generally take some portion of his theory or an element to which he did not give sufficient attention and magnify its relative significance, often to the point of caricature. While the outlines of method and of theory can be stated more or less simply, the details, which depend on human vicissitudes, remain necessarily complex.

The structure of Freud's theory encompasses at least two quite different spheres of interest, and these have not always been well differentiated. On the one hand, the theory is the assembled group of formulations about the treatment process, derived from the psychoanalytic method as it has gradually evolved. This extremely large group of propositions, to which many besides Freud have contributed in the past seventy-five years, is the field from which the analyst makes his selections in conceptualizing his clinical data. On the other hand, the theory encompasses a description of the human mind. I make more sparing use of this aspect of the theory in the immediacy of the clinical situation, but it informs my participation in the free association method and guides my interventions from a distance. The two spheres of theoretical interest have, of course, many points of intersection—not least among them the formulation of psychopathology. It would be helpful, I believe, for analysts to know how much or how little they use a theory of the mind in addition to a theory of the psychoanalytic process and to distinguish between the two.

It is in any case necessary, explicitly or implicitly, to have a theoretical formulation of the free association method from both aspects, as it appears in the psychoanalytic process and as a function of the human mind. That is, each analyst must in some way link the method he uses with a conception of the patient's mental life and the laws that govern its development, its organization, its functions, its relationship to the patient's body and to the outside world, and its accessibility to influence.

Bibliography

Arlow, J. A., and Brenner, C. (1964), *Psychoanalytic Concepts and the Structural Theory.* New York: Int. Univ. Press.

Blum, H. P. (1976), Acting out, the psychoanalytic process, and interpretation. *Annu. Psychoanal.*, 4:163–184.

——— ed. (1979), Psychoanalytic technique and theory of therapy. *J. Amer. Psychoanal. Assn. Suppl.*, 27.

Brenner, C. (1974), On the nature and development of affects: a unified theory. *Psychoanal. Quart.*, 43:532–556.

Breuer, J., and Freud, S. (1893–1895), Studies on hysteria. S.E.,* 2.

Dewald, P. A. (1978), The psychoanalytic process in adult patients. *Psychoanal. Study Child.* 33:323–332.

Freud, A. (1965), Normality and pathology in childhood. *The Writings of Anna Freud*, 6. New York: Int. Univ. Press, 1965.

——— (1968), Acting out. *The Writings of Anna Freud*, 7:94–109. New York: Int. Univ. Press, 1971.

Freud, S. (1894), The neuro-psychoses of defence. S.E., 3:43–68.

——— (1900), The interpretation of dreams. S.E., 4 and 5.

——— (1905), Fragment of an analysis of a case of hysteria. S.E., 7:3–122.

——— (1909), Notes upon a case of obsessional neurosis. S.E., 10:153–318.

——— (1913), Totem and taboo. S.E., 13:ix–161.

——— (1915), Instincts and their vicissitudes. S.E., 14:109–140.

——— (1917), Mourning and melancholia. S.E., 14:239–258.

——— (1923), The ego and the id. S.E., 19:3–66.

——— (1924), A short account of psycho-analysis. S.E., 19:191–209.

The Standard Edition of the Complete Psychological Works of Sigmund Freud, 24 Volumes. London: Hogarth Press, 1953–1974.

—— (1925), An autobiographical study. *S.E.*, 20:3—74.

—— (1926), Inhibitions, symptoms and anxiety. S.E., 20:75—175.

—— (1931), Letter 258, February 7, 1931, to Stefan Zweig. In: *Letters of Sigmund Freud*, ed. E. L. Freud. New York: Basic Books, 1960, pp. 402—403.

—— (1940), An outline of psycho-analysis. *S.E.*, 23:141—207.

Friedman, L. (1978), Trends in the psychoanalytic theory of treatment. *Psychoanal. Quart.*, 47:524—567.

Gedo, J. E., and Goldberg, A. (1973), *Models of the Mind*. Chicago: Univ. Chicago Press.

Gray, P. (1973), Psychoanalytic technique and the ego's capacity for viewing intrapsychic activity. *J. Amer. Psychoanal. Assn.*, 21:474—494.

—— (1981), "Developmental lag" in the evolution of technique for psychoanalysis of neurotic conflict. *J. Amer. Psychoanal. Assn.*, in press.

Greenacre, P. (1959), Certain technical problems in the transference relationship. In: *Emotional Growth*. New York: Int. Univ. Press, 1971, Vol. 2, pp. 651—669.

Greenson, R. R. (1967), *The Technique and Practice of Psychoanalysis*. New York: Int. Univ. Press.

Griesinger, W. (1845), *Mental Pathology and Therapeutics*. London: New Sydenham Society, 1867.

Hartmann, H. (1964), *Essays on Ego Psychology*. New York: Int. Univ. Press.

—— Kris, E., and Loewenstein, R. M. (1964). *Papers on Psychoanalytic Psychology*. [*Psychological Issues*, monogr. 14]. New York: Int. Univ. Press.

Hendrick, I. (1958), *Facts and Theories of Psychoanalysis*. New York: Knopf.

Hermann, I. (1934), *Die Psychoanalyse als Methode*, 2nd ed. Cologne: Westdeutscher Verlag, 1963.

Hoffer, W. (1950), Three psychological criteria for the termination of treatment. *Int. J. Psychoanal.*, 31:194—195.

Jacobson, E. (1964), *The Self and the Object World*. New York: Int. Univ. Press.

Johnson, S. (1750), Letter Number 2, Saturday, March 24, 1750. *The Rambler*. London: T. Longman et al., 1794, vol. 1, pp. 8—14.

Kanzer, M. (1958), Image formation during free association. *Psychoanal. Quart.*, 27:465—484.

—— (1961), Verbal and nonverbal aspects of free association. *Psychoanal. Quart.*, 30:327—350.

Kernberg, O. F. (1976), *Object Relations Theory and Clinical Psychoanalysis*. New York: Jason Aronson.

Klein, G. S. (1976), *Psychoanalytic Theory*. New York: Int. Univ. Press.

Kohut, H. (1966), Forms and transformations of narcissism. *J. Amer. Psychoanal. Assn.*, 14:243–272.

Kris, A. O. (1976), On wanting too much: the "exceptions" revisited. *Int. J. Psychoanal.*, 57:85–95.

———— (1977), Either-or dilemmas. *Psychoanal. Study Child*, 32:91–117.

———— (1979), Persistence of denial in fantasy. *Psychoanal. Study Child*, 34:145–154.

———— (1981), On giving advice to parents in analysis. *Psychoanal. Study Child*, 36, forthcoming.

Kris, E. (1975), *Selected Papers of Ernst Kris*. New Haven and London: Yale Univ. Press.

Lewin, B. D. (1973), Dream psychology and the analytic situation. In: *Selected Writings of Bertram D. Lewin*. New York: Psychoanalytic Quarterly, 1973, pp. 264–290.

Loewald, H. W. (1980), *Papers on Psychoanalysis*. New Haven and London: Yale Univ. Press.

Loewenstein, R. M. (1982), *Practice and Precept in Psychoanalytic Technique: Selected Papers of Rudolph M. Loewenstein*. New Haven and London: Yale Univ. Press, forthcoming.

Mahler, M. S., Pine, F., and Bergman, A. (1975), *The Psychological Birth of the Human Infant*. New York: Basic Books.

Mahony, P. (1979), The boundaries of free association. *Psychoanalysis and Contemporary Thought*, 2(2):151–198.

Rangell, L. (1954), Similarities and differences between psychoanalysis and dynamic psychotherapy. *J. Amer. Psychoanal. Assn.*, 2:734–744.

———— (1963a), The scope of intrapsychic conflict. *Psychoanal. Study Child*, 18:75–102.

———— (1963b), Structural problems in intrapsychic conflict. *Psychoanal. Study Child*, 18:103–138.

Rapaport, D. (1944), The scientific methodology of psychoanalysis. In: *The Collected Papers of David Rapaport*, ed. M. M. Gill. New York: Basic Books, 1967, pp. 165–220.

Ritvo, S. (1978), The psychoanalytic process in childhood. *Psychoanal. Study Child*, 33:295–305.

Sachs, D. M. (1979), On the relationship between psychoanalysis and psychoanalytic psychotherapy. *J. Phila. Assn. Psychoanal.*, 6:119–145.

Sandler, J., Kennedy, H., and Tyson, R. L. (1975), Discussions on transference. *Psychoanal. Study Child*, 30:409–441.

———— (1980), *The Technique of Child Psychoanalysis: Discussions with Anna Freud*. Cambridge: Harvard Univ. Press.

Schafer, R. (1976), *A New Language for Psychoanalysis*. New Haven and London: Yale Univ. Press.

———— (1978), *Language and Insight*. New Haven and London: Yale Univ. Press.

Spruiell, V. (1979), Freud's concepts of idealization. *J. Amer. Psychoanal. Assn.*, 27:777–791.

Stone, L. (1961), *The Psychoanalytic Situation*. New York: Int. Univ. Press.

Ticho, E. A. (1972), Termination of psychoanalysis: treatment goals, life goals. *Psychoanal. Quart.*, 41:315–333.

Waelder, R. (1962), Psychoanalysis, scientific method, and philosophy. *J. Amer. Psychoanal. Assn.*, 10:617–637.

Winnicott, D. W. (1958), *Collected Papers*. New York: Basic Books.

———— (1965), *The Maturational Processes and the Facilitating Environment*. New York: Int. Univ. Press.

Zetzel, E. R. (1970), *The Capacity for Emotional Growth*. New York: Int. Univ. Press.

Index

Abstinence, rule of, 44−45, 51
Adolescence: conflicts of ambivalence, 53−54, 96. See also Conflicts of ambivalence
Ambivalence. See Conflicts
Anonymity: analyst's responsibility for, 23−24; in analysis of unconscious guilt, 44−45
Arlow, J. A., 41
Authority: of analyst in free association, 22, 23, 24, 25−26

Blum, H. P., xi, 71
Boredom: as consequence of repression, 20
Brenner, C., 41, 42n
Breuer, J., x, 4

Child analysis: free association in, 94−95
"Chimney sweeping," x
Conflicts: fee and schedule, 29; intrasystemic, 53, 54
—of ambivalence: masturbation as,15; Freud's use of term, 53; loving and being loved, 53−54; in adolescence, 53−54, 96; scope, 54−55; either-or dilemmas, 55−56; "should" and "ought," 55−56; measures to resolve, 57−58; defense conflicts compared, 58−60; seen as states of loss, 59; mourning in, 59−60
—of defense: resistance analyzed in, 52; ambivalence conflicts compared, 58−60
Continuity: psychoanalytic method geared to identify, 6; alternative lines of, 6−7, 14−15
Couch: effects of use of, 101−02
Countertransference, 70. See also Transference

Daffodils, 8
Defenses; analysis of, 52
Definitions: method of free association, 3; reluctance, 31; resistance, 31, 33; mourning, 59−60; transference, 61−63, 65−66, 68, 70; process of free association, 71
Dewald, P. A., 71
Discontinuities. See Continuity

Ego, intrasystemic conflicts in, 54
Either-or dilemmas, 55−56
Externalization, 26−27, 49. See also Unconscious guilt

Fantasies: perverse, 19−20, 33; acting out, 28; ambivalent wishes in, 54; adolescent, 92. See also Conflicts of ambivalence
Fees and schedules: analyst's responsibilities, 29
Free association: as point of departure for formulation, ix, xi, 1, 2, 5, 61, 70, 71, 103−05; directed, x; Freud's use of, x; psychopathology as limiting, 4, 15; freedom of, 9; forms of, 10−12, 95; aim of, 14; influences on, 40−41; intervention, 49; reluctance to pursue, 73−76, 94; developmental context of, 94−97
—activity of: described, 8−9, 39; satisfaction in, 34, 47−49, 50−51; in conflicts of ambivalence, 57−59; in psychoanalysis and psychotherapy, 100
—functions of: stated, 14; remembrance as, 14, 21; in therapeutic process, 71
—method: as central point of reference, 2; defined, 3; formulation of, 22; responsibilities of analyst in,

111